DIY Couture

CREATE YOUR OWN FASHION COLLECTION

Rosie Martin

LAURENCE KING PUBLISHING

LAURENCE KING

Published in 2012 by Laurence King Publishing Ltd
361–373 City Road
London EC1V 1LR
United Kingdom
Tel: + 44 20 7841 6900
Fax: +44 20 7841 6910

e-mail: enquiries@laurenceking.com
www.laurenceking.com

A catalogue record for this book is available from the British Library.

ISBN: 978-1-85669-799-6

Design: Eleanor Ridsdale
Senior Editor: Clare Double
Senior Commissioning Editor: Helen Rochester

All artworks and step-by-step photography by Rosie Martin
Model Photography: Simon Pask
Make-up Artist: Karen Fundell
Styling: Rosie Martin
Wardrobe Assistants: Alexandra Bickerdike, Arliyah Hussain, Rosie Kavanavoch, Roshni Patel

Printed in China

Thank you
Special thanks to my endlessly supportive Mum and Dad, to Hannah my super sister, to the one and only Joel Timothy Shea, to Angela Hooker who has donated time, energy and ideas to DIYcouture from the very beginning, to my brilliant friend Louise Rondel and to my band BAANEEX.

CONTENTS

I. INTRODUCTION 6

II. YOU WILL NEED 8

III. USEFUL TECHNIQUES 10

01_ Straight stitch 11
02_ Hemming 11
03_ Zigzag stitch 12
04_ Bias binding 14
05_ How to make pockets 16
06_ How to make belt loops 18
07_ How to make straps 19

The garments made in eight collections:
01_ Acid Candy 20
02_ Monochrome Art 21
03_ American Road Trip 22
04_ Rude Disco 23
05_ Coffee Classic 24
06_ Jungle Punk 25
07_ Safari Prep 26
08_ Tea Picnic 27

IV. THE INSTRUCTIONS 28

01_ The straight skirt 30
02_ The Grecian dress 46
03_ The skater skirt 60
04_ The waistcoat 76
05_ The cloak 90
06_ The slouch top 108
07_ The goddess dress 124
08_ The hoody 146
09_ The trousers 168
10_ The romper 186

Templates 204
Sewing resources 206
Styling 207
About the models 208

I.

introduction

A NOTE ABOUT SEWING

Welcome to this bumper book of DIYcouture instructions. The picture-based instructions in this book have sprung from my desire to help make sewing accessible to anyone and everyone.

Sewing is a visual activity: making clothes is simply a process of binding big flat sheets of colour together to create something three-dimensional. You do not need years of training or instinctive skills to be able to make a piece of clothing that is good-looking, wearable and durable. I believe that getting stuck in is the best way of learning, so the instructions in this book aim to help you get going and make something you are proud of.

A key message I would like to put across is: don't worry too much about the details. No doubt, making things 'accurately' will make you feel good about the item you have made. However, when you wear shop-bought clothes, it is unlikely that you zoom in on the fine points of their construction. When you try on a new piece of clothing and look in the mirror, you generally do not look at whether a line of stitching is straight, or the buttons are sewn on perfectly evenly. You look at how the garment hangs on your body; you think about how it feels; you look at the colour or pattern of the fabric. When you see a dress you like on someone in the street, you are probably not admiring the amazingly even seam depth.

Next time you are in a high-street clothing shop, or even a vintage or designer boutique, take a moment in the changing room to focus on a hem, a strap or a join. You will probably start to notice things that you would criticize if you had done them yourself. All the clothes pictured in this book were handmade at home, and very few of them could be considered 100% perfect. My line of reasoning is this – let it go. Those small details do not matter to a garment's looks or usability.

Through making any or all of the ten garments set out in this book, I hope that you will not only craft your own clothes and love wearing them, but that you will also develop an understanding of the general principles of garment construction. By going through the basic motions of making, I hope that you will gain the confidence to problem-solve when it comes to sewing in general.

DIY Couture

One of the guiding principles of making clothes is that you have an inside and an outside. The inside – or 'wrong' side – is where you tuck away all your unkempt edges. You can use your inside to hide anything messy that you don't want the world to see. When you start to think about how you can use the inside to make a tidy, presentable outside, you can start to work out how to build your own garments from scratch.

HOW TO USE THE INSTRUCTIONS

All the projects are illustrated with step-by-step diagrams and photographs of each piece made in the Acid Candy style. Two different ways of marking and cutting shapes are used in this book; you may find one or the other simpler. The instructions for the **cloak** (pages 90–107), **skater skirt** (pages 60–75) and **goddess dress** (pages 124–145) require you to begin with nothing more than a couple of simple measurements, which are then used to mark out basic geometric shapes (e.g. a circle or a rectangle). You may find this method the most inviting. It is perhaps more prescriptive, or less risky, as it asks you to make very few decisions, and no creative drawing is required. The instructions for the **Grecian dress** (pages 46–59), **slouch top** (pages 108–123), **straight skirt** (pages 30–45), **hoody** (pages 146–167), **trousers** (pages 168–185) and **romper** (pages 186–203) ask you to use clothing that you already have to draw some simple outlines. The **waistcoat** instructions (pages 76–89) are a hybrid of these two methods.

If you are very new to clothes-making, it can be satisfying to begin by constructing something fairly quickly. The skater skirt, Grecian dress and waistcoat have the fewest steps and are therefore the least time-consuming to make. The romper and the hoody have the most steps and require more time.

The measurements given on the 'technical variations' pages will help you compare the different versions. Don't worry about very precise measurements. This is sewing the DIY way.

I hope that the combination of drawings, photographs and words used here guides you through the making process and supports you in creating garments that you enjoy both putting together and wearing. I hope you find the photos of different models wearing different versions of the garments made in a range of fabrics inspiring and that these images help you to kindle your own ideas of what you would like to create.

Happy sewing.

Rosie Martin

II.

you will need

There are a few basic items that you need to sew your own clothes. All the garments photographed in this book were handmade at home using just the simple pieces of equipment listed here.

FABRIC

FABRIC

Making clothes is really a practical way of displaying a piece of fabric that you love. The properties of the fabric you choose will strongly influence the feel, the look and the hang of the garment you make. Many fabrics have a 'right' side, which is meant to be shown to the world, and a 'wrong' side. Throughout this book the right side of the fabric is indicated in the illustrations with a more intense colour. The wrong side is shown in a paler colour. The amount of fabric you need for each garment will depend on your size and how you want your garment to look. For instance, if you are making the cloak (pages 90–107), you may want to make a tiny shoulder cape, or you may prefer a long winter cloak that hangs down to your knees. Before you go fabric shopping, read through the 'technical variations' section for your chosen garment. This section illustrates eight different versions of the garment, including descriptions of the differences between them, which will help you decide how you want your garment to appear. As a general rule, 3m (118in) of fabric is a generous amount that will allow you to make almost anything. Wash and iron fabric before sewing, as some fabric shrinks when washed.

FABRIC SCISSORS

FABRIC SCISSORS

Get yourself a pair of fabric scissors. Cheap ones will work fine; more expensive ones will probably last you forever. Look after your scissors – don't cut paper with them, as it will blunt the blades and they will then snag your fabric.

TAILOR'S CHALK

TAILOR'S CHALK

You can buy tailor's chalk in the form of a flat, soapy triangle or as a pencil. Either will do. Tailor's chalk allows you to make marks on your fabric that easily brush or wash off. Rub the tailor's chalk on in short, firm strokes while pressing the fabric down with your free hand to keep it steady.

SEWING MACHINE

THREAD

BOBBINS

QUICK UNPICK

IRON

SEWING MACHINE

You can make professional, long-lasting garments with just two types of stitch: straight stitch and zigzag stitch. These two basic stitches are found on nearly all sewing machines. You will only need these two stitches to make the garments in this book. There are various brands of domestic sewing machines available, but all have a very similar standard set-up. If you have access to a friend's or relative's machine, try it out to see if you like it. Most likely, you will grow to love whichever machine you purchase.

THREAD

You need to choose a thread that is a similar colour to your fabric. This will help you worry less about whether your lines of stitches are straight – if the stitches are camouflaged, it doesn't really matter if they are uneven. Take a cutting of your fabric with you when you buy your thread. If you can't find an exact match, choose a thread that is slightly darker than your fabric.

BOBBINS

Your sewing machine should come with a few empty bobbins, made of plastic or metal. You need to wind thread onto these yourself. Your sewing machine's instruction booklet will tell you how to do this.

QUICK UNPICK/SEAM RIPPER

You can't expect to get everything right first time. You may stitch up an edge that should be left open, or sew some of your fabric inside out. Making mistakes when you sew is frustrating because it takes more time to undo them than it does to make them in the first place. Luckily, you can rely on your friend the quick unpick tool to help you get the job done. Just slip the long metal spike under your unwanted stitch and push. The curved metal crook will slice through your thread. You can cut every fourth or fifth stitch and gently pull your fabric apart to speed up the process.

IRON

An iron is an essential tool when it comes to making clothes. It is almost as important as your sewing machine.

III.
useful techniques

01.

straight stitch

PAGE 11

02.

hemming

PAGE 11

03.

zigzag stitch

PAGE 12

04.

bias binding

PAGE 14

05.

pockets

PAGE 16

06.

belt loops

PAGE 18

07.

straps

PAGE 19

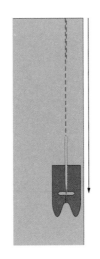

1_ Position your needle a little 'inland'.

2_ Sew a short line of straight stitch in reverse.

3_ Sew forwards, directly over the line you have just sewn.

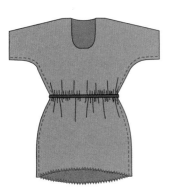
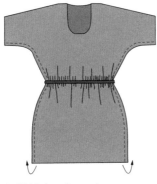

1_ Zigzag over the raw edge.

2_ Fold the edge under.

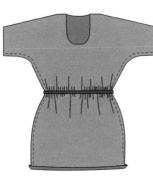

3_ For delicate fabric, turn once…

4_ …then turn again to conceal the hemmed edge.

01_STRAIGHT STITCH

When your machine sews straight stitch, it simply pushes thread in and out of your fabric in a long line. If you were to pull the thread at one end of your row of stitching, you could begin to work it loose. You need to prevent this from happening and can do so very simply.

Your machine sews naturally 'forwards', towards you, as if it is gently chomping your fabric and excreting it out behind it. Whenever you begin a row of straight stitch, you will naturally wish to start sewing at the far edge of your fabric. However, you need to **position your needle a couple of centimetres 'inland'** (1). With your needle so positioned, put your machine foot down and set your machine to sew backwards. **Cover this distance in reverse with a short line of straight stitch** (2).

When your needle is at the far edge of the fabric, you can begin to **sew forwards, directly over the line you have just sewn** (3). This will hold the stitches in position and ensure you make strong, long-lasting garments. When you finish your line of straight stitch, sew backwards a couple of centimetres too, over the top of your last few stitches, to hold them in place.

02_ HEMMING

Hemming is simply a way of finishing a straight raw edge. The goal is to hide the unfinished edge on the inside of your garment. Hemming is usually the last thing you do to finish a garment.

Run over your raw edge with zigzag stitch so the fabric won't unravel (1). With your garment turned inside out, **fold the zigzagged edge over** on itself a small amount, just 1 or 2cm (⅜in–¾in) (2). You should be looking at a thin, fairly even, strip of fabric about that deep running all the way around or along the edge you are hemming.

You can iron the hem into place before you sew, or just dive straight in to securing the hem with a line of straight stitch. You will need to insert the arm of your sewing machine into your garment. If you have made a very skinny sleeve end or trouser leg, you will have to do a bit of hand-stitching.

If your fabric is quite delicate and you think zigzagging might chew up the raw edge, you can **make two folds instead of one**, (3, 4) so that your raw edge is completely hidden. This kind of hem is also useful in cases where the inside of the garment may sometimes show. For this reason, it is used on the bust part of the goddess dress, shown on pages 136–137.

Hems can be used to make a channel through which elastic can be threaded. You can use elastic in this way to give a garment shape. This technique is used in the trousers and romper instructions.

03_ ZIGZAG STITCH

The purpose of zigzag stitching is to prevent the strands of fibre that make up your fabric from unravelling. Have a look at the edge of one of your fabric pieces and rub it gently between your thumb and finger. You will probably see some fibres beginning to show their ends. To prevent them from unravelling, you need to bind them into place with zigzag stitch.

When your sewing machine needle sews zigzag stitch, it moves from left to right to left to right (1–4). When you position your fabric on your machine, you need to place it so that the needle hits the fabric when it moves to the left, but hits air when it moves to the right; i.e., you only want half of the zigzag to land on your fabric. This means that instead of just sitting on your fabric, the stitch **almost wraps around the edge of your fabric** (5), binding the fibres and preventing any loose ones working themselves free. Having said this, don't worry if the odd stitch falls completely on your fabric – your garment won't suddenly fall apart as you walk down the street. The more you sew, the more accurate you will become.

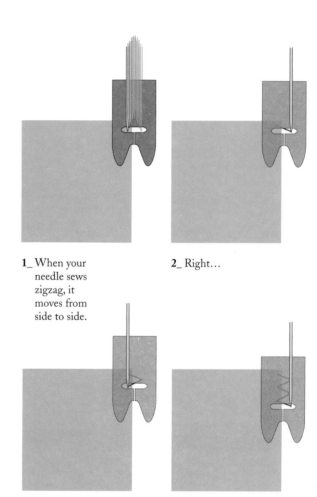

1_ When your needle sews zigzag, it moves from side to side.

2_ Right...

3_ Left...

4_ Right...

5_ Zigzag stitch wraps around the edge of your fabric.

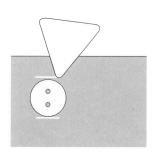

1_ Mark each side of the button.

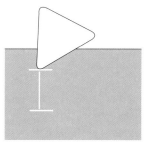

2_ Draw a line between the marks.

3_ Sew down one line.

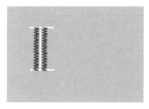

4_ Continue along the other side.

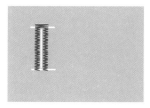

5_ Sew wide stitches at one end of the buttonhole.

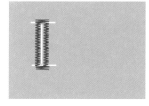

6_ Do the same at the other end.

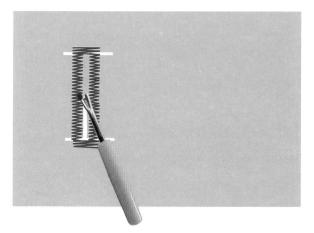

7_ Slice through the fabric to create a buttonhole.

Using zigzag stitch to make a buttonhole

You can make a secure and fairly tidy buttonhole very simply using zigzag stitch.

Work out where you would like your buttonhole to sit and rest your button there. **Make a mark on either side of your button** (marking the longest distance across it) with tailor's chalk (1). Remove your button and **draw a straight line between the two marks you have made** (2). You are going to encase this line with a rectangle of zigzag stitching and then slice your fabric along the chalk line.

Set your machine to sew a narrow zigzag stitch, and also so the zigzags fall closely together. You need to squash the normal concertina of zigzag stitches so that very little fabric shows between each stitch. **Sew down one long side of your chalk line** with this narrow, squashed-up zigzag stitch (3). You will be making almost one thick, solid line of stitching. **Sew down the other long side** of your chalk line with the same stitch (4). Ideally, there will be just 2 or 3mm (⅛in) between the two lines, but don't worry if it is slightly more.

Now set your zigzag stitch so that it is as wide as possible. My sewing machine sews a zigzag stitch of a maximum 7mm (5/16in) wide. Leave your stitch so that it is still set to sew squashed up, so your stitches land almost on top of one another. **Now sew a few stitches back and forth at each end of your chalk line**, making ends for your rectangle of stitches (5, 6).

Now take your seam ripper and **jam it into your fabric at one end of the chalk line** (7). Push it carefully so that it slowly slices through your fabric, stopping just before you reach the stitches at the other end. You have made a buttonhole.

04_ BIAS BINDING

Using bias binding is a simple way of finishing a curved edge. Curved edges cannot be hemmed simply by folding over a flap of fabric in the way that straight edges can. Bias binding is a strip of fabric that has been cut diagonally – that is, on the bias. This means the strip of fabric will bend, even if there is no stretch in the original fabric. The bend will allow you to completely cover – or 'bind' – raw curved edges.

Bias binding can be shop-bought, and comes in many colours. It is often a little stiff. If you want a bias binding that is exactly the same pattern and weight of your garment, you can make your own from the fabric of your choice. There is a handy tool called a bias tape maker that makes this process extremely easy. You can buy one on the internet.

If you want to dive in and make your bias binding without waiting for the tool to arrive, that is possible too – it just takes a little patience.

How to make bias binding

Begin with a piece of fabric that has straight edges and square corners – a square or a rectangle. The strip you are going to cut needs to run diagonally across your fabric. Fold one corner of your fabric up and **run a piece of fabric chalk across the fold**, marking the diagonal edge (1). Now unfold the corner and flip your fabric over so you can see the chalk mark.

Decide how deep you would like your bias binding to appear on your finished garment. You need to cut your strip of fabric four times this depth. For example, if you want 1cm (⅜in) of bias binding to show at the front of your garment, you need to cut a strip 4cm (1½in) wide. **Make a second chalk line** running parallel to your first, to your required distance (2). Cut along your chalk lines. Trim the ends of your strip so they have flat ends.

Your bias binding needs to be slightly longer than the curved edge you wish to cover. Measure the length of that edge with a piece of string.

Now measure the strip you have cut. Is it as long as the length of bias binding you need? If not, don't worry; you just need to cut multiple strips of fabric until they all add up to make the length you need. Mark as many parallel lines on your fabric as you will need, then **cut along your lines** (3).

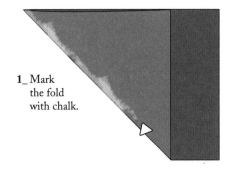

1_ Mark the fold with chalk.

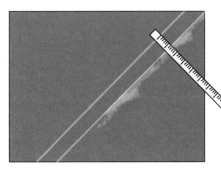

2_ Make a second line parallel to the first.

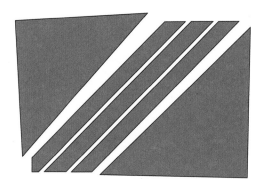

3_ Cut as many strips as you need.

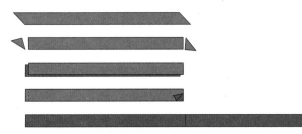

4_ Joining two strips of fabric.

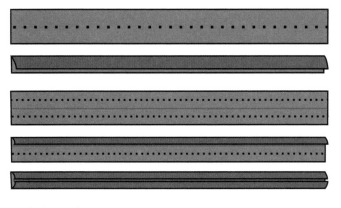

5_ Folding and ironing a strip.

6_ A cross-section of your bias binding would look something like this.

7_ Put the bias binding in place.

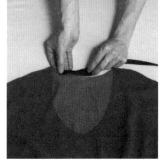

8_ Fold the bias binding over to encase the edge.

9_ Trim the end to allow a little overlap.

10_ Sew the end neatly in place.

If you do need to **join multiple strips of fabric**, you can do it by taking two strips and laying them one on top of the other. Pin and stitch one end, iron the edges flat and turn right way up before using (4).

Take your strip of fabric and fold it in half longways, ironing the fold into place. You are now going to fold your strip into quarters. Open it up and fold one edge towards the crease you have made, so that it falls just a couple of millimetres short. Iron this folded edge. Repeat this with the other edge. You now have a **strip of fabric with three creases ironed in** (5). When you fold all the creases up, you have a thin strip of fabric with neatly finished edges (6).

Your bias binding is ready to go.

Your bias binding needs to **sit over the raw edge of your fabric**, so one half sits behind the fabric and one half sits in front (7). You will **sandwich your raw edge** so that it is completely encased by the bias binding (8). Position one end of your bias binding like this and put it under your sewing machine foot. Sew slowly along your bias binding, positioning it so that it encases the raw edge as you go. As you sew, try to be aware of the shape of the edge you are covering. You want to keep this shape, so try not to stretch it out so that it makes a straight line. Try to keep the garment in shape as you sew.

When you get all the way back to where you started, **trim your bias binding** so there is a slight overlap (9). Sew the end over the beginning of the bias binding (10). You can sew over this with a little bit of zigzag stitch for ultra-neatness.

05_ HOW TO MAKE POCKETS

To make a pocket, first **cut a rectangle** (a). The one here is about half the height of the skirt and just over half the width. **Trim any one of the corners** so that it is curved (1). You are going to cut a curved indent into your shape. This will be where your hand goes into the pocket. To get roughly the right shape, put two pins into the horizontal edge of your piece to **divide it more or less into thirds** (2). Do the same with one vertical edge. Now **cut away a curve** that eats up two-thirds of the horizontal edge and one-third of the vertical edge (3, b).

This is your first pocket piece. Use it as a template to **cut a mirror image of the same shape** for your other pocket (4). Use these two pieces to **cut two pieces of lining fabric** exactly the same (5).

Lay your lining piece out with the right side of the fabric facing upwards towards you and **lay your outer fabric on top** of it with the right side facing down (6). **Pin** (7). Sew the outer to the lining, **leaving one straight edge unsewn** (8). **Trim both curved areas of your pocket,** the concave and the convex (9). This will help you to make a smooth, flat edge when you turn your pocket inside out. **Trim your corners** diagonally too (10). This will help you create sharp corner points. Put your hand into the unsewn end of your pocket and **turn it the right way round** (11, c).

Iron the edges flat (d). **Turn the unsewn edge** in on itself (e) and iron it flat (f).

a_ Cut a rectangle of material.

b_ Cut away a curve at the top.

c_ Turn the pocket inside out.

d_ Iron all the edges flat.

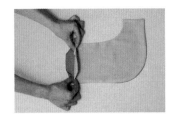
e_ Turn the free edge inwards.

f_ Iron the edge flat.

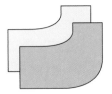
1_ Trim one corner.

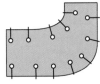
2_ Divide the edges into thirds.

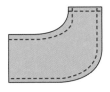
3_ Cut away the top of the pocket.

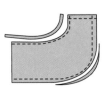
4_ Cut the second pocket.

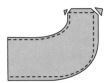
5_ Cut out the lining pieces.

6_ Lay out a pocket and a lining piece.

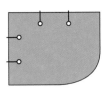
7_ Pin these together.

8_ Sew together, leaving one edge free.

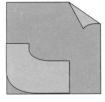
9_ Trim the edges.

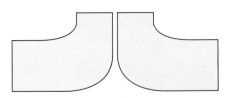
10_ Trim the corners.

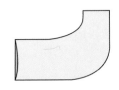
11_ Turn the pocket right way out.

g_ Pin in place.

h_ Sew the pocket on.

i_ Tug the pocket upwards…

j_ …to add volume.

k_ Pin the back of the pocket.

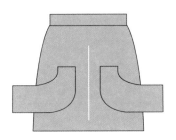

l_ Look at the back to judge where to pin the second pocket.

Find the centre of your garment. **Mark the centre of your garment** either by drawing a line with tailor's chalk or by laying your tape measure or a piece of string down the central axis (12). Use this to help you visually **place your pockets evenly on either side** (13).

Pin your first pocket to your garment along the top straight edge and the curved bottom edge (g). **Sew along these edges,** but stop your line of stitching before you get to the side seam of your garment. Leave about 5cm (2in) at the front unsewn (h).

Lay your garment out again and **tug the pocket upwards,** pivoting it on the end of the line of stitches you just made (i). This **gives your pocket some volume,** rather than it sitting flat against your garment (j). Now **pin the unsewn part of your pocket** (14), continuing right round the back of your garment (15, k). Sew these pinned edges down (16). You have made a working pocket.

Repeat this process on the other side of your garment (17).

When it comes to spinning your garment round so you can pin the back of your pocket, look at the amount of pocket fabric that sticks out from the side of your garment and use this to help you judge where to **pin your second pocket** (l).

12_ Mark the centre of your garment.

13_ Gauge the position of your pockets.

14_ Add volume to the pocket and pin in place.

15_ Continue pinning at the back.

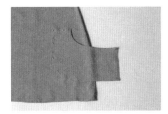

16_ Stitch the back of the pocket.

17_ Repeat with the second pocket.

06_ HOW TO MAKE BELT LOOPS

You can make a simple belt loop from just a small rectangle of fabric. You can make the loops to match your garment or from a fabric that contrasts to add a splash of colour.

First, put your garment on and fasten the belt of your choosing over your garment, wherever you intend it to sit. **Put a pin into your garment** above the belt and one below (1). Do this on both sides at the front of your body and once on the back (in the middle), if you can.

Now take your garment off and lay it out.

Use your tape measure to **measure the distance between the upper and lower pins** (2). Add an extra 4cm (1½in) to this, and then measure this distance up the vertical side of the fabric you have chosen for your belt loops and mark with a pin.

Work out how wide you would like your belt loop to be and measure double this distance plus an extra 1.5cm (⅝in) along the bottom, horizontal edge of your fabric. Mark with another pin. Use these pins to cut out a small rectangle of fabric. Use this rectangle as a guide to cut out as many more pieces as you need for the number of belt loops you are making.

Fold your first rectangle in half with the right side of the fabric hidden on the inside (3). Pin the fold into place, then sew along the edge of the piece with straight stitch **to make a short tube** (4).

Put your fingers into the tube and pull it inside out so you are looking at the right side of your fabric (5). Flatten out your belt loop so the seam sits slightly to one side and iron the whole thing flat. Run over each short end with a line of zigzag stitch, then fold over about 1cm (⅜in) of fabric at each short end. **Iron the fold flat** (6).

Place the belt loop onto your garment, in line with your pins. Pin it into place (7), then **sew over the folded edge with straight stitch**, onto your garment (8). You have made a belt loop. Repeat this process for the other side of your garment.

1_ Pin where your belt will sit.

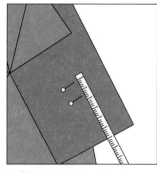

2_ Measure between the pins.

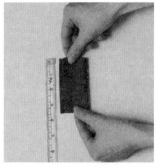

3_ Fold the first loop in half.

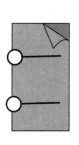

4_ Sew the edge to make a tube.

5_ Pull the tube inside out.

6_ Iron the ends flat.

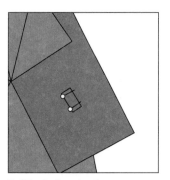

7_ Pin the loop in place.

8_ Sew on using straight stitch.

07_ HOW TO MAKE STRAPS

A strap can be made very simply from a strip of fabric, and joined to your garment after you have made it.

Put your garment on and drape a tape measure over your shoulder. Dangle the zero end of the tape measure over to your back so the zero is hovering roughly at the edge of your garment. Now look at the measurement at the top edge of your garment at the front. You need to make your straps a few centimetres longer than this. We'll call this your length measurement.

Measure your length measurement up the vertical edge of your fabric. Mark this distance with a pin. Now measure double the width you would like your strap to be, plus an extra 3cm (1¼in) across the horizontal edge of your fabric. Mark this with a pin. Cut into your fabric from your pins to make a long rectangle.

Fold your rectangle in half lengthways with the right side of the fabric hidden on the inside of the fold (1). Match up the straight edges of the fabric and **pin them together** (2). **Sew your pinned edge** with a line of straight stitch running about 1.5cm (⅝in) from the edge (3). You now have a long tube of fabric. **Turn the whole tube inside out** (4). You should be looking at the right side of your fabric and your seam should be hidden on the inside of the tube.

Flatten the tube with the seam sitting slightly over to one side and **iron it flat** (5). Run a line of zigzag stitch across each short end. Repeat to make a second strap.

Position one end of your first strap where you would like it to sit (6). Tilt the strap slightly. This will help it to sit flat on your shoulder. The **arrow on the diagram** indicates this tilt (7). You can try the garment on and put a pin in to mark where you want the strap to sit.

Sew your strap to the top edge of your garment. Position your second strap in roughly the same place on the other side of your garment, then pin and **sew it into place** (8).

Try your garment on inside out and check your straps are the right length. If they are, you can lay your garment out again, fold the straps over and pin the unattached ends into place at the back. Sew the ends of your strap into place with short lines of straight stitch (sitting above and below the channel if you are making a romper). You have made some straps.

Bear in mind that for the romper (pages 186–203), the fabric will be scrunched up a little, so the straps will be drawn into the centre further than where you position them. The straps on your romper need to straddle the channel you have left for threading elastic through. Position the strap so you will be able to sew one line of straight stitch at the top of the channel and one line underneath it.

1_ Fold in half. 2_ Pin. 3_ Sew the edges. 4_ Turn inside out.

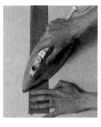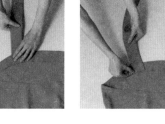

5_ Iron flat. 6_ Consider where to place the first strap.

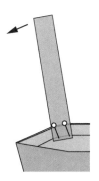

7_ Tilt the strap. 8_ Sew both straps in place.

01.

the acid candy collection

THE STRAIGHT SKIRT   THE GRECIAN DRESS   THE SKATER SKIRT   THE WAISTCOAT   THE CLOAK

THE SLOUCH TOP   THE GODDESS DRESS   THE HOODY   THE TROUSERS   THE ROMPER

02.

the monochrome art collection

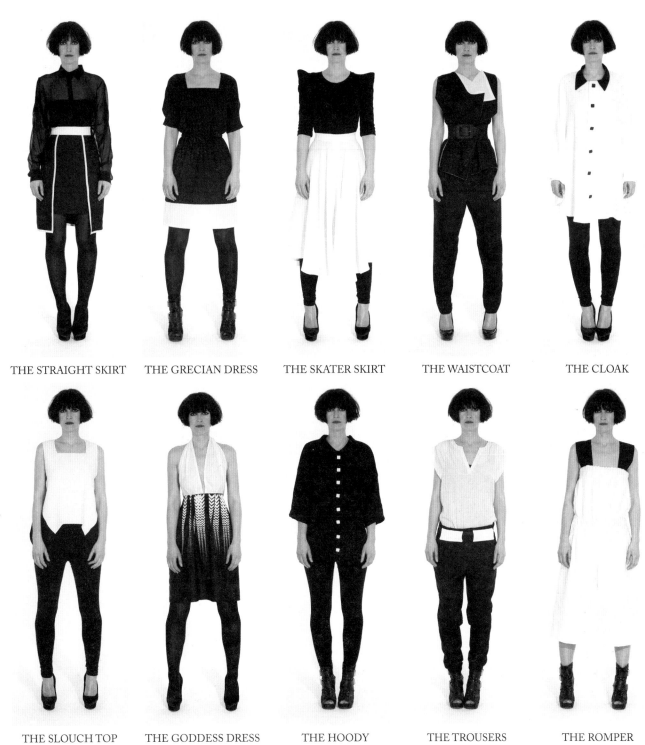

THE STRAIGHT SKIRT · THE GRECIAN DRESS · THE SKATER SKIRT · THE WAISTCOAT · THE CLOAK

THE SLOUCH TOP · THE GODDESS DRESS · THE HOODY · THE TROUSERS · THE ROMPER

03.

the american road trip collection

THE STRAIGHT SKIRT   THE GRECIAN DRESS   THE SKATER SKIRT   THE WAISTCOAT   THE CLOAK

THE SLOUCH TOP   THE GODDESS DRESS   THE HOODY   THE TROUSERS   THE ROMPER

04.

the rude disco collection

THE STRAIGHT SKIRT   THE GRECIAN DRESS   THE SKATER SKIRT   THE WAISTCOAT   THE CLOAK

THE SLOUCH TOP   THE GODDESS DRESS   THE HOODY   THE TROUSERS   THE ROMPER

05.

the coffee classic collection

THE STRAIGHT SKIRT

THE GRECIAN DRESS

THE SKATER SKIRT

THE WAISTCOAT

THE CLOAK

THE SLOUCH TOP

THE GODDESS DRESS

THE HOODY

THE TROUSERS

THE ROMPER

06.

the jungle punk collection

THE STRAIGHT SKIRT THE GRECIAN DRESS THE SKATER SKIRT THE WAISTCOAT THE CLOAK

THE SLOUCH TOP THE GODDESS DRESS THE HOODY THE TROUSERS THE ROMPER

07.

the safari prep collection

THE STRAIGHT SKIRT

THE GRECIAN DRESS

THE SKATER SKIRT

THE WAISTCOAT

THE CLOAK

THE SLOUCH TOP

THE GODDESS DRESS

THE HOODY

THE TROUSERS

THE ROMPER

08.

the tea picnic collection

THE STRAIGHT SKIRT   THE GRECIAN DRESS   THE SKATER SKIRT   THE WAISTCOAT   THE CLOAK

THE SLOUCH TOP   THE GODDESS DRESS   THE HOODY   THE TROUSERS   THE ROMPER

IV.

the instructions

01.

the straight skirt

PAGES 30 — 45

02.

the grecian dress

PAGES 46 — 59

03.

the skater skirt

PAGES 60 — 75

04.

the waistcoat

PAGES 76 — 89

05.

the cloak

PAGES 90 — 107

06.

the slouch top

PAGES 108 — 123

07.

the goddess dress

PAGES 124 — 145

08.

the hoody

PAGES 146 — 167

09.

the trousers

PAGES 168 — 185

10.

the romper

PAGES 186 — 203

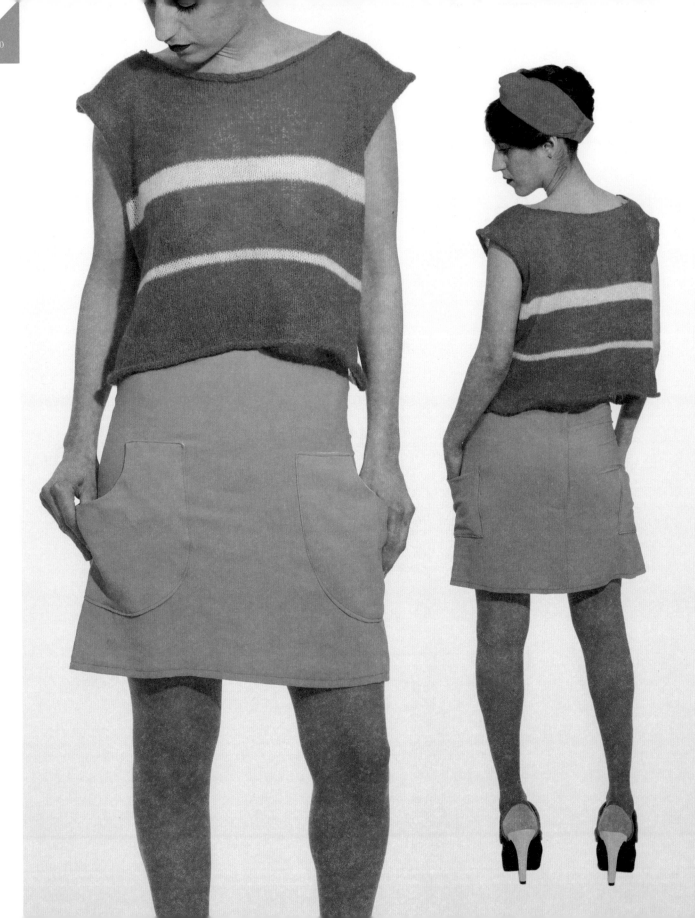

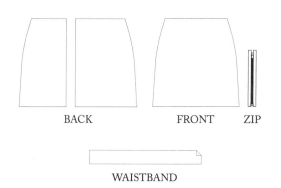

BACK   FRONT   ZIP

WAISTBAND

01.

the straight skirt

The straight skirt is a simple, figure-hugging skirt. It is made of three main pieces of fabric, with one extra strip that forms the waistband. The skirt fastens with a zip at the front or the back. Two pockets can be added to create a dramatic shape.

TECHNICAL VARIATIONS
the straight skirt can be made and worn in a variety of ways

1_ ACID CANDY

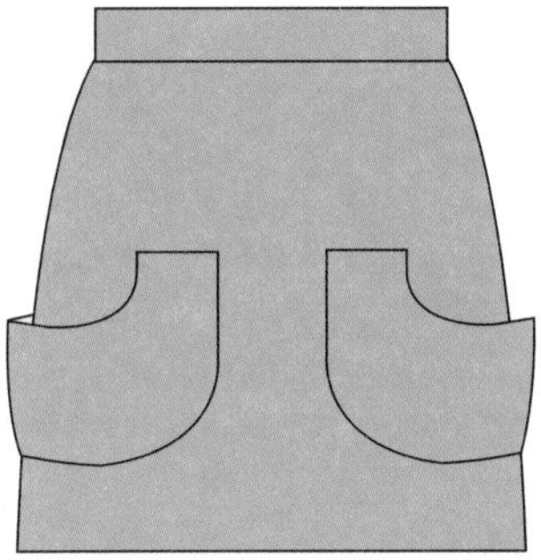

2_ MONOCHROME ART

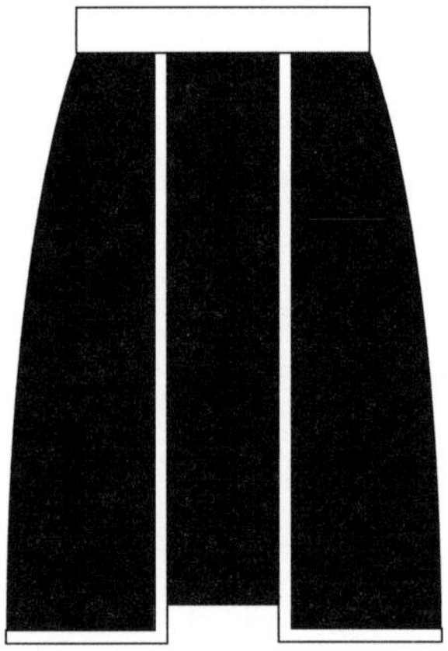

3_ AMERICAN ROAD TRIP

4_ RUDE DISCO

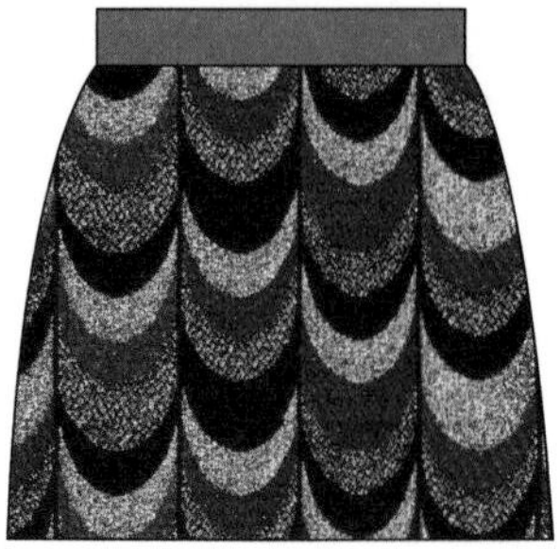

5_ COFFEE CLASSIC

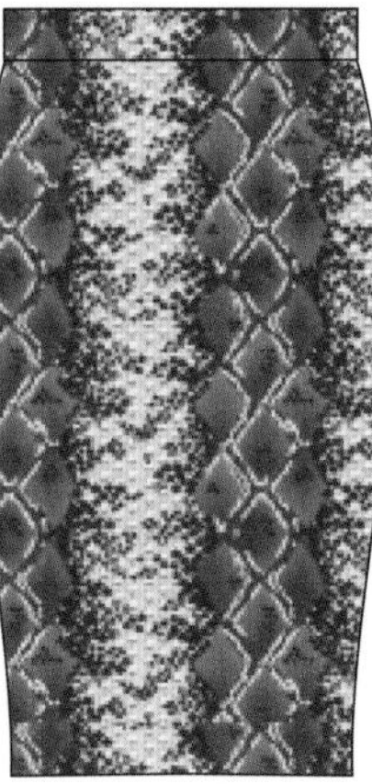

6_ JUNGLE PUNK

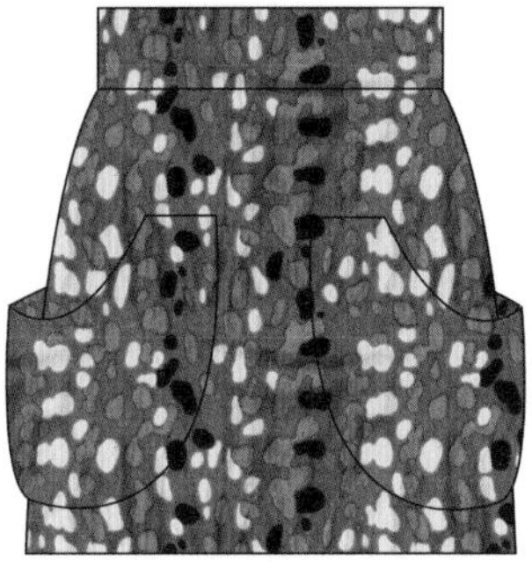

7_ SAFARI PREP

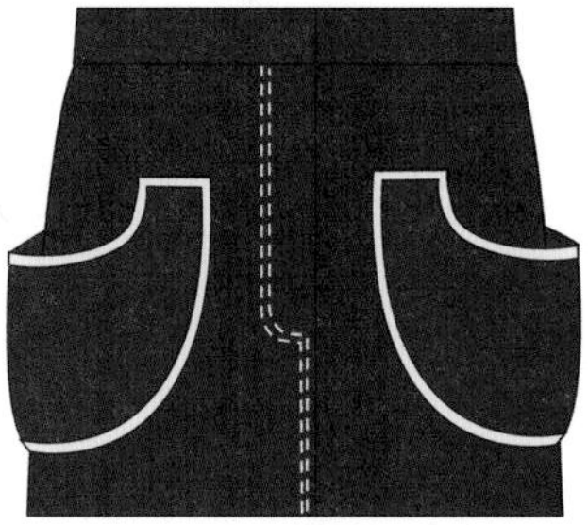

8_ TEA PICNIC

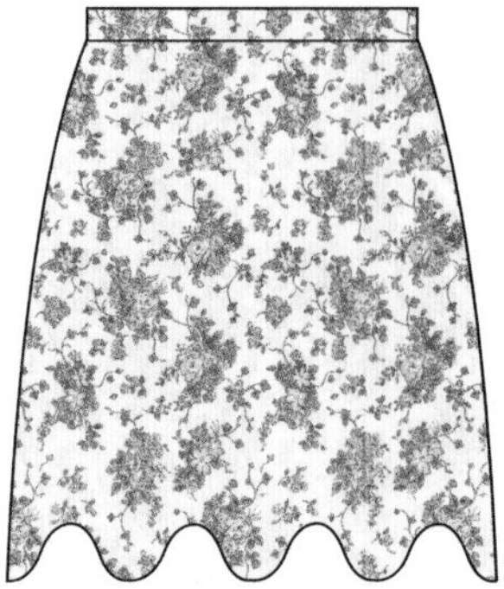

1_ ACID CANDY

The Acid Candy straight skirt is made of a floppy synthetic fabric. The skirt has a fairly slim 4cm (1½in)-deep waistband and fastens at the back with a zip. It falls above the knee and has two deep side pockets that are lined in a pale polycotton. The pockets are 23cm (9in) deep. The pockets and the length of the skirt give the garment a casual feel.

2_ MONOCHROME ART

The Monochrome Art straight skirt is made of a floppy suiting fabric and has a waistband of white polycotton. The finished waistband is 4.5cm (1¾in) deep. The shape at the front of the skirt is made by attaching a decorative panel at each side. The initial front piece for the skirt is marked and cut, then used to cut a piece the same shape but shorter. The initial front piece is then cut in two down the centre. These two pieces are trimmed to make them slimmer. Each panel is then edged with white bias binding and sewn on top of the right side of the short front piece, before attaching this piece to the back.

3_ AMERICAN ROAD TRIP

The American Road Trip straight skirt is made with a thick, stiff denim. It has a deep waistband of 7.5cm (3in). The skirt has no zip, instead fastening at the front with a row of buttons. Rather than leaving a gap for the zip, each separate side of the skirt is hemmed all the way from top to bottom, and the two sides overlap each other at the front. Buttonholes are added to one hemmed side and buttons to the other. The skirt has no flare in it. The shape of the initial front piece is altered by trimming the sides.

4_ RUDE DISCO

The Rude Disco skirt is made using light but stiff second-hand curtain fabric. The skirt is very short. The pieces are cut 38cm (15in) long. The skirt fastens at the back with a zip.

5_ COFFEE CLASSIC

The Coffee Classic straight skirt is made using fabric that has a significant stretch. The skirt pieces are cut 57cm (22½in) long. The skirt is sewn so that it clings to the body at the top and the seams at each side are made to slope slightly inwards to give the skirt more of a pencil shape than an A-line shape. The skirt has a 6cm (2.5in)-deep waistband.

6_ JUNGLE PUNK

The Jungle Punk straight skirt is made using a fairly stiff patterned cotton. The skirt is short and has two deep pockets – the pocket pieces were cut 25cm (10in) deep. The waistband is fairly deep, at 6cm (2½in). The skirt fastens at the back with a zip.

7_ SAFARI PREP

The Safari Prep straight skirt is made of a medium-weight maroon suiting with quite a rough texture. The skirt has two pockets made of extremely stiff navy polycotton. Due to the stiff nature of this fabric, the pockets stick right out like wings. Instead of using two layers of fabric to create neat pocket edges, these pockets are made with one layer of fabric and their edges finished with bias binding. This skirt has a 5cm (2in)-deep waistband and, although it is fairly short, measuring 36cm (14in) before the waistband is added, it is made to sit on the hips rather than the waist. The skirt fastens at the front with a zip.

8_ TEA PICNIC

The Tea Picnic skirt is made using thin printed polycotton. It has a slim 3cm (1¼in)-deep waistband and fastens at the back with a zip. The bottom is shaped into scallops. This is done before the front and the back of the skirt are sewn together, by sewing a shaped lining to the outside of the fabric and then turning it to the inside and ironing the edge flat.

To begin, get a pair of shorts or trousers that fit you snugly. If you only have trousers that sit on your hips, put them on and hold the zero end of your tape measure at the top of your waistband. Let the tape measure hang down. Stand in front of a mirror. Think about where you want your skirt to hang and look at the measurement there. Write the number down. We'll call this your **length measurement**.

Measure the distance between the waistband of the trousers and your actual waist (the thinnest part around your middle). It may help if you tie a piece of yarn or string around your waist, so that you can see the line you need to measure to/from. Write down this measurement. We will call this your **waist-to-hip measurement**.

Then measure the full distance around your waist and write that number down. We'll call that your **full waist measurement**.

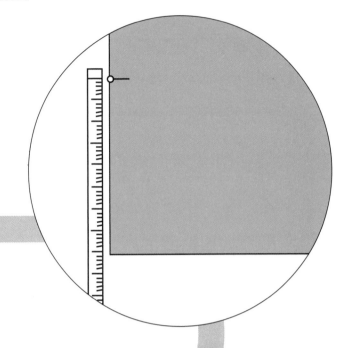

1_ Lay out your fabric flat on the floor. Measure your length measurement from the bottom edge of your fabric upwards and put a pin in here.

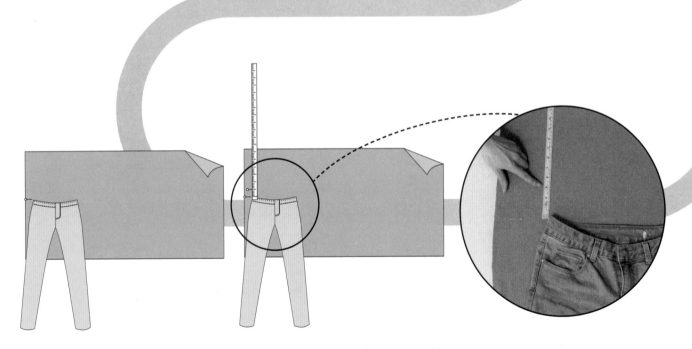

2_ Take the trousers you have chosen and lay them on your fabric so that the top of the waistband is in line with the pin you put into your fabric.

3_ If you are using trousers that sit on your hips, measure your waist-to-hip measurement upwards from the place you have put a pin and put another pin in there.

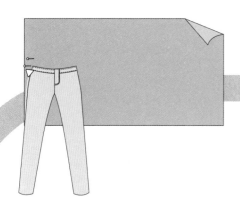

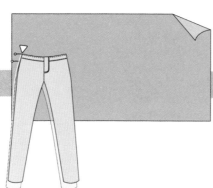

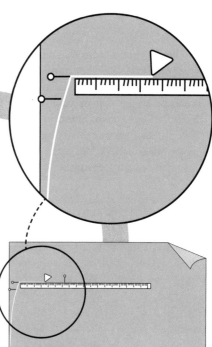

4_ Use your trousers as a guide to draw the shape of your skirt with tailor's chalk, making your marks about 1.5cm (⅝in) away from the edge of your trousers.

5_ Now shift your trousers upwards to your top pin (if using) so you can use them as a guide to continue your chalk line.

6_ Measure half of your full waist measurement, plus an additional 4cm (1½in), horizontally across your fabric from the top of your chalk line, and put a pin in there. While your tape measure is laid out, use it as a guide to draw a straight line across your fabric from pin to pin with chalk.

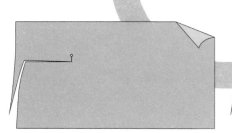

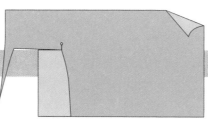

This is the front of your skirt.

7_ Cut out the left side of your skirt and cut at least halfway along the horizontal line.

8_ Fold this cut half over to the right and use it as a guide to cut the second half exactly the same, so you have a perfectly symmetrical shape.

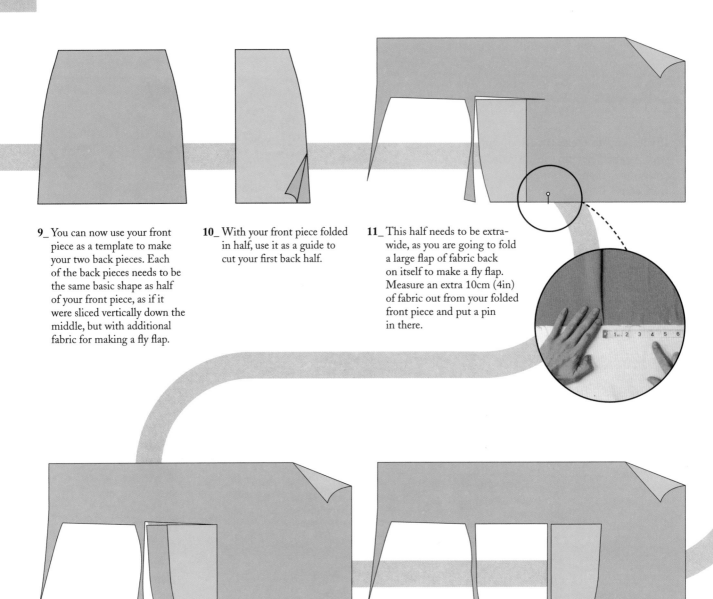

9_ You can now use your front piece as a template to make your two back pieces. Each of the back pieces needs to be the same basic shape as half of your front piece, as if it were sliced vertically down the middle, but with additional fabric for making a fly flap.

10_ With your front piece folded in half, use it as a guide to cut your first back half.

11_ This half needs to be extra-wide, as you are going to fold a large flap of fabric back on itself to make a fly flap. Measure an extra 10cm (4in) of fabric out from your folded front piece and put a pin in there.

12_ Cut up the curved side of your skirt, then shift your front piece across so the vertical edge meets the pin on your fabric. Use the folded edge to guide you in cutting a straight line.

13_ Flip your folded front piece over and use it again as a template to cut the second back half. This half just needs to have an additional 1.5cm (⅝in) width to make a hem.

If you want to make the Monochrome Art straight skirt with a raised hemline in the centre section, you need to create the shaped front piece now before continuing from step 14.

a_ Once you have cut your front piece, lay it on your fabric with the end over the edge. Use it as a guide to cut a piece the same shape, but shorter.

c_ Cut a section from the straight edge of each half.

b_ Cut your longer front piece in half down the centre.

d_ Trim the edges with white bias binding.

e_ Matching up the side edges of the trimmed pieces and the short front piece, sew together.

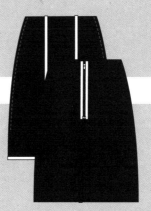

f_ Add a zip to the back piece (see step 14 onwards) and sew front and back together.

g_ The finished skirt.

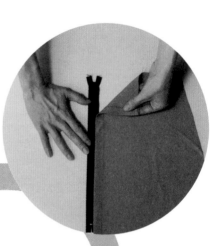

14_ Zigzag-stitch down each of the straight vertical edges of your back pieces to prevent them from fraying. Then take your narrower back piece and fold back the zigzagged edge by 1.5cm (⅝in). Iron this flap flat.

15_ You are now going to attach this piece to your zip. Lay your zip out on the floor with the back piece on top of it, with the neat edge you have just ironed running along the vertical edge of your zip. You should be looking at the right side of your fabric, with the folded edge hidden at the back.

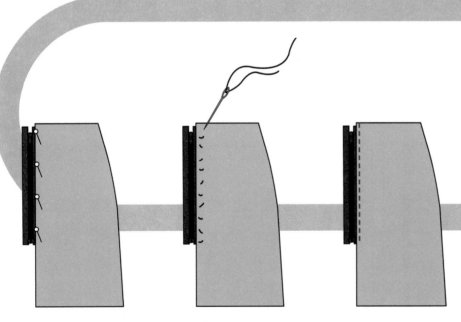

16_ Pin the piece into place then roughly hand-sew the piece to the zip.

17_ Machine-sew the fabric to the zip with a line of straight stitch.

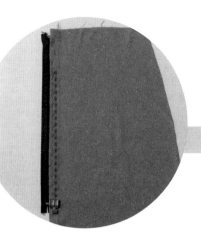
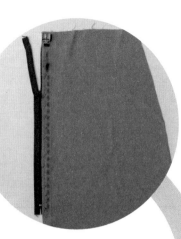

18_ Start with your zip foot positioned below your zip's pull tab and sew down to the bottom.

19_ Then unzip your zipper about halfway and position your foot right at the top of your zip. Sew down until you meet the top of the line of stitches you just made.

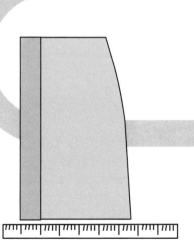
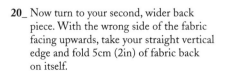
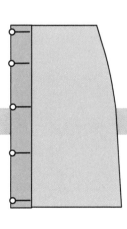
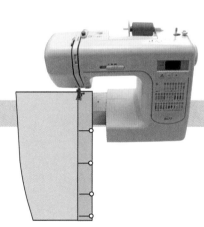

20_ Now turn to your second, wider back piece. With the wrong side of the fabric facing upwards, take your straight vertical edge and fold 5cm (2in) of fabric back on itself.

21_ You should be looking at a 5cm (2in)-wide strip of the right side of your fabric running vertically all the way up your shape. Iron the flap, then pin it into place.

22_ Stitch the flap down close to your zigzagged edge with a long straight stitch that you can easily unpick later if you want to.

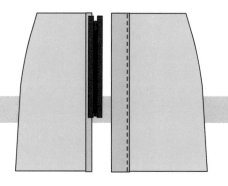

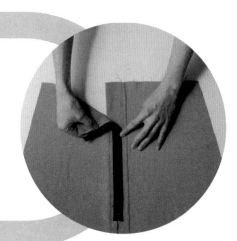

23_ Lay your two back pieces out with the wrong sides facing upwards.

24_ Drag the half with the zip attached on top of your half with the fly flap, so that the unattached edge of the zip just about meets the zigzagged edge of your fly flap.

25_ Pin the zip into place. Roughly hand-stitch it and remove the pins.

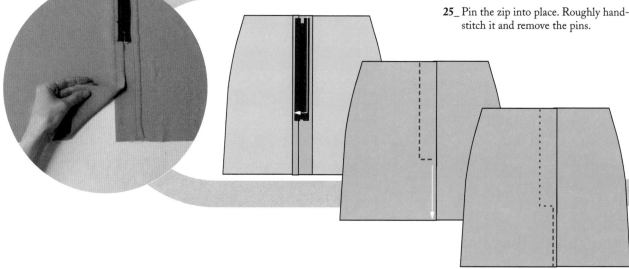

26_ Machine-sew down the side of the zip, then turn the corner and sew across the bottom of the zip while you are looking at this side of the fabric (so you can see the zip).

27_ Cut your thread, then flip your piece over and continue sewing to the bottom of your skirt while looking at this side.

You have made a neat and discreet zip fly and have a complete back piece. If you would like to make a scalloped edge as seen on the Tea Picnic straight skirt, go to page 185 for instructions. Now it's time to join your back piece to your front piece.

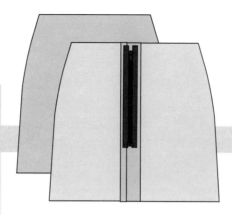
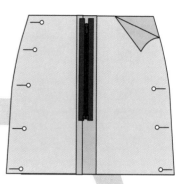

28_ Lay your front piece out with the right side of the fabric facing upwards and lay your back piece on top of it with the right side facing down.

29_ Pin the two pieces together up each side. If your back piece is slightly wider than your front piece, don't worry – just trim the sides until the pieces are equal. Sew the pieces together with straight stitch, then, with your skirt still turned inside out, try it on for size.

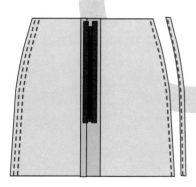

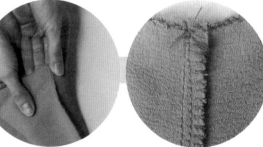

30_ Now is the time to get the waist of your skirt fitting accurately. If it is too baggy, sew lines of straight stitch equally further inland at both sides of your skirt until it is the right size. Trim off the excess material.

31_ Neaten the side seams of your skirt by zigzagging over each edge, then folding it to one side and stitching over it so the flap is held flat.

Now you need to make your waistband piece. This needs to be slightly longer than the full distance around the waist edge of your skirt.

32_ Measure the waist edge, then add 8cm (3¼in) to this to allow for a button flap and for hems.

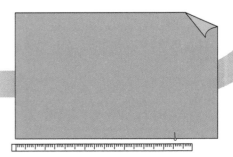

33_ Mark out that length along your fabric.

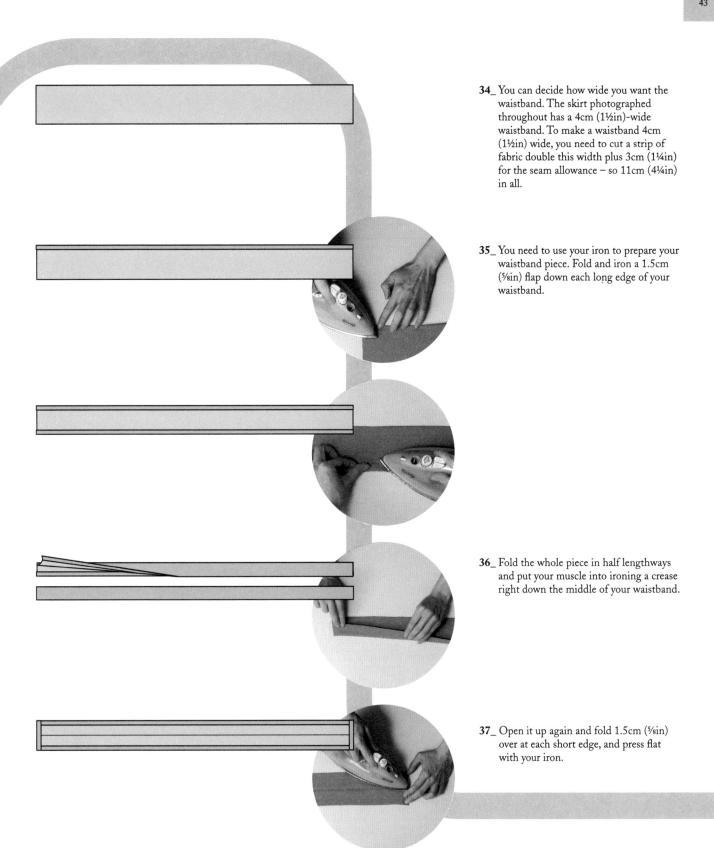

34_ You can decide how wide you want the waistband. The skirt photographed throughout has a 4cm (1½in)-wide waistband. To make a waistband 4cm (1½in) wide, you need to cut a strip of fabric double this width plus 3cm (1¼in) for the seam allowance – so 11cm (4¼in) in all.

35_ You need to use your iron to prepare your waistband piece. Fold and iron a 1.5cm (⅝in) flap down each long edge of your waistband.

36_ Fold the whole piece in half lengthways and put your muscle into ironing a crease right down the middle of your waistband.

37_ Open it up again and fold 1.5cm (⅝in) over at each short edge, and press flat with your iron.

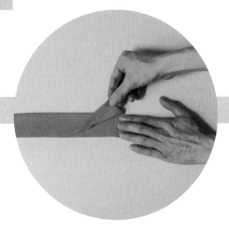

38_ Close the whole piece up again and press the ends with your iron.

39_ You are now going to attach your waistband piece to your skirt. You will encase the waist edge of your skirt with your waistband so that the raw edge is hidden. Take one of the short edges of your waistband and line it up with one of the neat zip edges that sits in front.

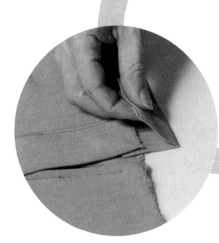

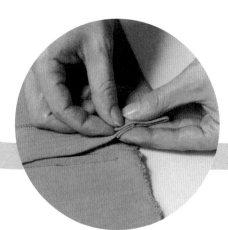

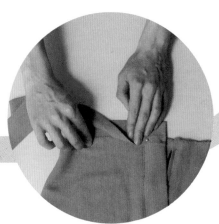

40_ You attach your waistband in a similar way to attaching bias binding (see page 14). You have a strip of fabric with a sort of spine, like a book. You use this hinged strip to encase the raw edge at the top of your skirt, front and back. When you fold the strip so it is completely snapped shut,

you will hide the raw edge and you will be able to sew all the way through the front of the strip, the edge you are encasing, and the back of the strip.

41_ Start pinning your waistband to your skirt. Use the ironed-in edge on the back flap of the waistband to help you; you can line up the top edge of the skirt with the edge of the ironed fold that you have made.

 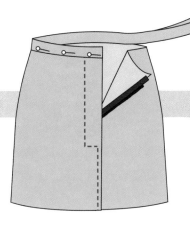 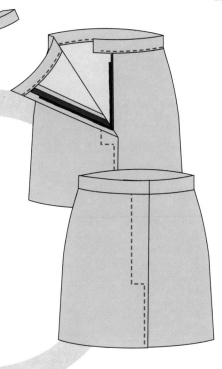

42_ Pin it into position so that the pin goes through the front of your waistband, your skirt, and the back of your waistband. Continue pinning like this all the way around your skirt.

43_ Sew the waistband into place with a line of straight stitch that catches the front of the waistband, the main skirt, and the back of your waistband.

Now hem the bottom edge of your skirt.

You can also add pockets to your skirt now if you like – see pages 16–17 for guidance on this.

you have made a straight skirt

44_ Your skirt is almost complete. Finally, you need to hand-sew a fastening to the top of your skirt on the waistband flap. You can use a press-stud, a hook and eye, or a button. See page 13 for how to make a buttonhole.

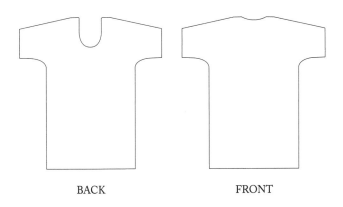

BACK   FRONT

02.

the grecian dress

The Grecian dress is a comfortable dress that fits loosely around the shoulders and can be brought in at the waist or hips with elastic or with a belt. The dress is simply made of two pieces of fabric that form the front and the back. There are no additional sleeve pieces.

TECHNICAL VARIATIONS

the grecian dress can be made and worn in a variety of ways

1_ ACID CANDY

2_ MONOCHROME ART

3_ AMERICAN ROAD TRIP

4_ RUDE DISCO

5_ COFFEE CLASSIC

6_ JUNGLE PUNK

7_ SAFARI PREP

8_ TEA PICNIC

1_ ACID CANDY

The Acid Candy Grecian dress is made from a thin, transparent chiffon that is floppy and quite delicate. The bias binding at the neck is handmade using purple polycotton (see page 14 for guidance on this). The waist of the dress is brought in by one thin 4mm (³⁄₁₆in)-wide piece of elastic, which is sewn fairly low in the dress so that the top of the dress flops over it. The front and back dress pieces measure 56cm (22in) across the bottom before they are sewn together.

2_ MONOCHROME ART

The Monochrome Art Grecian dress is made from floppy black suiting fabric. A thick strip of white fabric is added to the bottom after the front and back are joined at one side. This dress has a square neckline, finished with a separate piece of black bias binding for each edge. The dress is brought in at the waist by a 2.5cm (1in)-wide piece of elastic that is sewn to the dress with two lines of stitching.

3_ AMERICAN ROAD TRIP

The American Road Trip Grecian dress is made using mock velvet. Velvet can take some patience to work with, as the dense pile can cause the needle to veer off in the wrong direction. This dress is finished at the neck with a navy blue bias binding. It has no waistband, creating a loose, comfortable tunic. The dress has longer sleeves than the Acid Candy version (the shoulder seam measures 50cm/20in from the neck edge to the sleeve tip); they almost touch the elbows. The template T-shirt was shifted further inland to achieve this.

4_ RUDE DISCO

The Rude Disco Grecian dress is made using a very floppy fabric that has a tone-on-tone stripe effect. The dress has very short sleeves. Both the sleeve ends and the neck have been finished with bias binding of different colours. The dress has a high waistband made from a thick, 5cm (2in)-deep strip of elastic. This causes the dress to cling to the chest, and there is very little overhang of fabric over the waist area. The piece has been made as a fairly short, fun mini-dress.

5_ COFFEE CLASSIC

The Coffee Classic Grecian dress is made from a heavy jersey-type metallic fabric that has a wrinkle effect due to being stored in a cupboard in a bundle for a very long time. The dress is an elegant maxi dress, cut extremely long so that it almost sweeps the floor. It is drawn in right under the bust in an empire-line shape, with a single skinny 4mm (³⁄₁₆in)-wide piece of elastic.

6_ JUNGLE PUNK

The Jungle Punk Grecian dress is made from a fairly stiff printed cotton. The dress has short sleeves and a scoop neckline that is both wide and deep. The dress perches just on the shoulders. The neckline has been finished with black bias binding. The dress is brought in at the waist with a single skinny piece of elastic. The dress has black cotton pockets added at the front to make the dress practical and to give it a utilitarian appearance.

7_ SAFARI PREP

The Safari Prep Grecian dress is made from a tough cotton with a strong graphic printed pattern. It has fairly long sleeves that are finished with black bias binding, as is the neckline, which has been cut into a V-shape. The dress is worn here with a belt, hugging it to the body.

8_ TEA PICNIC

The Tea Picnic Grecian dress is made from a gingham printed polycotton. It has a low waistband made from a 2cm (¾in)-wide strip of elastic that sits on the hips. The dress is a comfortable, daytime length, the bottom hem falling just below the knees. The neckline is wide but shallow, creating a slash rather than a scoop effect.

To draw the correct shape for your dress, you need a couple of measurements and a T-shirt that fits you loosely. A man's T-shirt is ideal for this.

The front piece of your Grecian dress will be similar to that of a man's T-shirt, but with a few variations. It will be longer, as it is a dress not a top. It will have a curve at the armpit rather than an angle. It will not change angle dramatically at the shoulder. It will be wider, so that your bottom can fit into it. The following instructions will guide you through a way of marking this shape. There is no need to worry about exact angles or precise measurements.

Get a tape measure and, standing in front of a mirror or with help from a friend, measure the length that you would like your dress to be, using your body as a guide. Put the zero point of your tape measure at your collarbone and let the tape measure hang down. Look at the measurement at the point where you want your dress to hang and write it down. We'll call this measurement your **dress-length**. Holding the tape measure in the same place, measure down to your waist and write down this measurement too. We'll call this your **waist-depth** measurement.

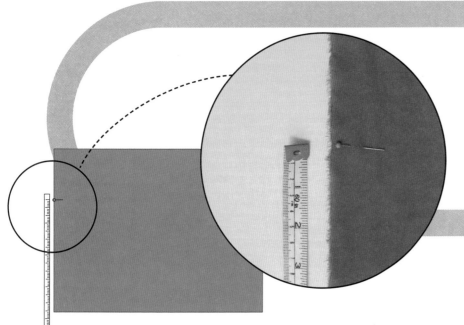

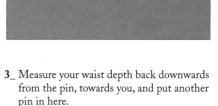

1_ Lay your fabric out flat on the floor with the right side facing upwards. Use your tape measure to measure your dress length along one vertical straight edge of your fabric.

2_ If you are adding elastic or intend to wear the dress with a belt, add an extra 10cm (4in) to this to allow for the fabric that will be gathered up. Put a pin in your fabric at this distance.

3_ Measure your waist depth back downwards from the pin, towards you, and put another pin in here.

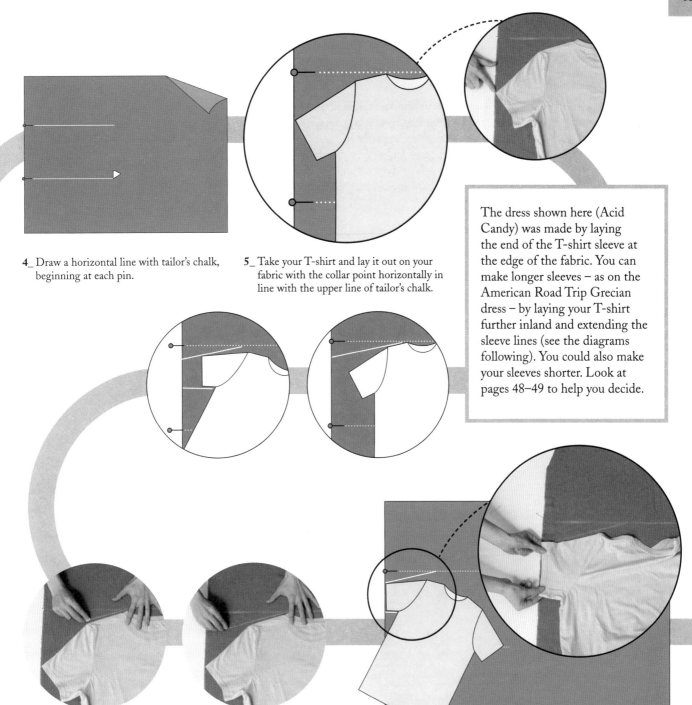

4_ Draw a horizontal line with tailor's chalk, beginning at each pin.

5_ Take your T-shirt and lay it out on your fabric with the collar point horizontally in line with the upper line of tailor's chalk.

The dress shown here (Acid Candy) was made by laying the end of the T-shirt sleeve at the edge of the fabric. You can make longer sleeves – as on the American Road Trip Grecian dress – by laying your T-shirt further inland and extending the sleeve lines (see the diagrams following). You could also make your sleeves shorter. Look at pages 48–49 to help you decide.

6_ Following your T-shirt, mark a sloping shoulder line with your tailor's chalk.

7_ Continue this line until you reach the edge of your fabric, ignoring any change of angle in your T-shirt.

8_ Now pull your T-shirt over so the straight end of the sleeve sits in line with the vertical straight edge of your fabric.

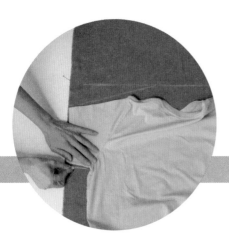

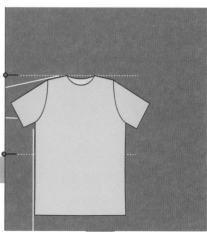

9_ Draw a line that will mark the underside of your sleeve.

10_ Now lay your T-shirt out straight again, as it was when you began, but shift it over to the right about 6 or 7cm (2½–2¾in). With your T-shirt still in this position, use the left vertical edge as a guide to mark the side of your dress shape.

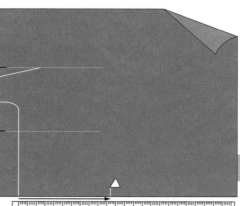

11_ You can put your T-shirt to one side. You have marked the underside of your sleeve and the vertical side of your dress. Join these together with a curved line. You are making a smooth, rounded, underarm curve.

12_ Your dress needs to hang comfortably round your bottom and hips, without clinging. Measure all the way around yourself at the widest point now. Halve this measurement and measure that distance across your fabric, marking it with chalk. As a guide, an extra 10cm (4in) must be added for the dress to hang comfortably.

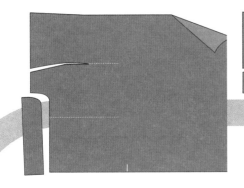 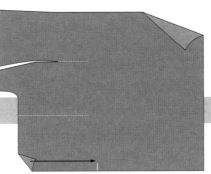 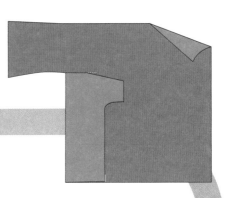

13_ Cut out the left half of your shape. You will be cutting up the straight, vertical side, under the curved armpit, along the top of your sleeve and straight across at the neck area.

14_ Fold your cut half over to the other side, matching up the bottom corner with the chalk mark you made.

15_ Cut around the folded half to make a perfectly symmetrical shape.

Now cut a curved neck shape.

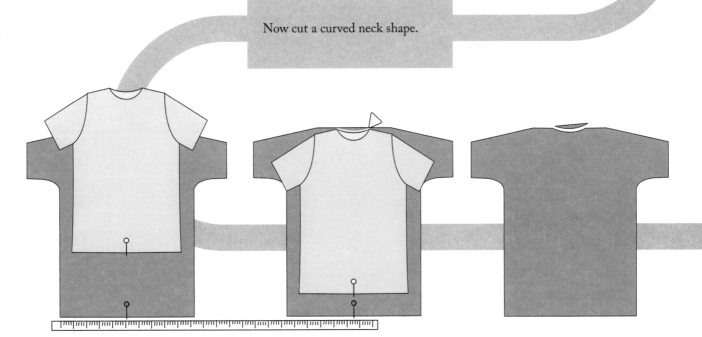

16_ Find the centre of your piece and the centre of your original T-shirt and put a pin in at both places.

17_ Lay the T-shirt on top of your garment piece, lining up the central pins. Use the curved neckline of the T-shirt to mark a similar line onto your fabric with chalk.

18_ Cut along the chalk line.

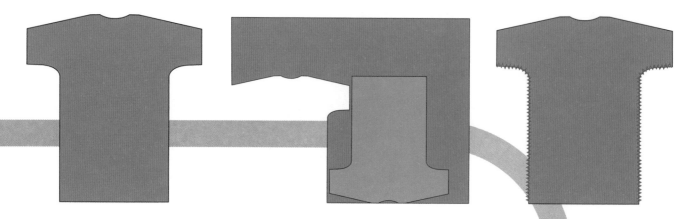

19_ You have made your first piece.

20_ With your first shape cut, use it as a guide to cut a second piece exactly the same.

21_ With two pieces cut, zigzag-stitch down both sides of each piece.

Now you can join your pieces together.

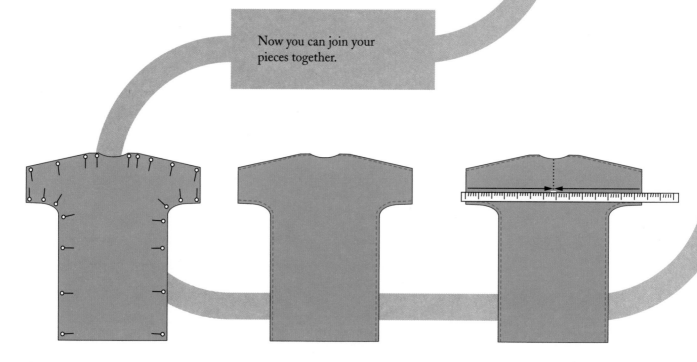

22_ Place one with the right side of the fabric facing upwards, and lay the second piece on top of that with the right side facing down. You should be looking at the wrong side of the fabric. Pin your two pieces together along the sloping shoulder edges and down both sides.

23_ Now sew your pieces together with straight stitch along the edges you have pinned, about 1.5cm (⅝in) away from the edge. You will be sewing along the shoulder edges on either side of your neck hole and down each side of your dress. Remove your pins as you sew.

24_ Your dress is shaping up, but at the moment you probably won't be able to push your head through the neck hole. You need to make the neck hole bigger so you can try the dress on. Start by finding the centre of your dress.

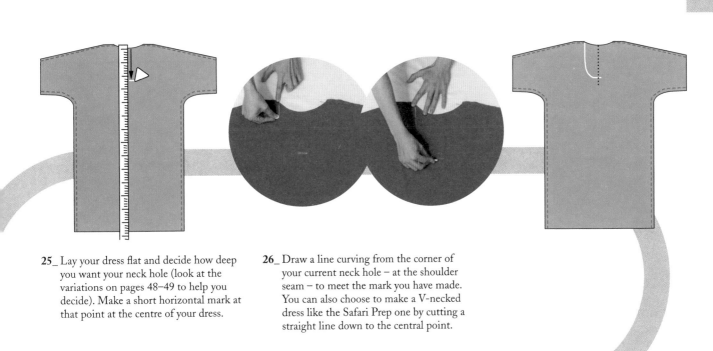

25_ Lay your dress flat and decide how deep you want your neck hole (look at the variations on pages 48–49 to help you decide). Make a short horizontal mark at that point at the centre of your dress.

26_ Draw a line curving from the corner of your current neck hole – at the shoulder seam – to meet the mark you have made. You can also choose to make a V-necked dress like the Safari Prep one by cutting a straight line down to the central point.

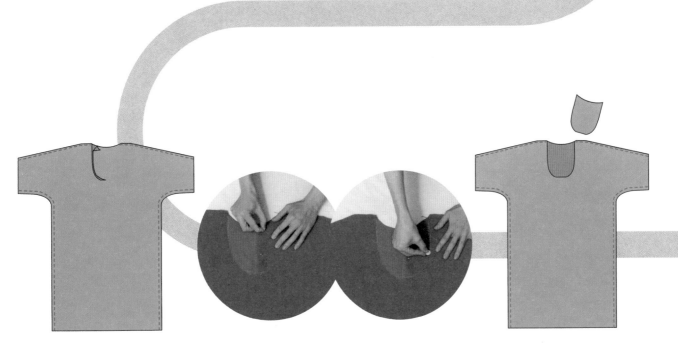

27_ Cut along the line you have drawn, to your central mark, then fold this flap of fabric over to the other side of your dress.

28_ Match the corner of the flap with the corner of your neck hole and pin the flap down.

29_ Use it as a guide to mark and cut a symmetrical neck hole.

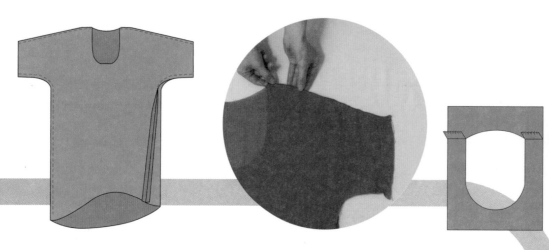

30_ Before you go any further, you need to sort out the seams of your dress. Open the flaps at your side seams and iron them open as much as you can. Iron this seam open at your sleeve ends too, until the armpit curve prevents you from going any further.

31_ Your shoulder seams are hard to access with an iron, but you can neaten them in a different way. Zigzag-stitch the flaps of fabric together, so that your stitches catch the front and back pieces, then push this one flap to the back of your dress.

33_ Turn your dress the right way round and put it onto your sewing machine so that the machine is sticking into the neck hole. You won't be able to see the flap of fabric, but feel it with your fingertips and make sure it is folded over to the side. Sew the flap down with a line of straight stitch running 2 or 3mm (⅛in) away from the line where your front and back pieces join. Your stitches should catch the folded flap and secure it flat.

32_ Sew the flap into this position.

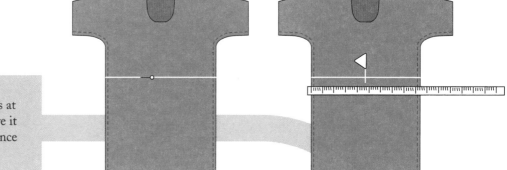

Now add elastic or belt loops at the waist of your dress to give it shape. See page 18 for guidance on making belt loops.

34_ To add elastic, turn your dress inside out and try it on. Look at the waistline you drew right at the start and see if it is positioned at the level you would like your dress to pinch your body. If you would rather the pinch were somewhere else, make a mark with chalk or add a pin at the point where you want it. Take your dress off and draw this horizontal line with chalk all the way around your dress. You will use this line as a guide when you sew the elastic into your dress.

35_ You also need to mark the centre of the line across the front of your dress and the centre of your line across the back, with either a pin or a short chalk mark.

You need to prepare your elastic before you start sewing.

36_ Take a strip of elastic and wrap it around your waist (or wherever the dress is going to pinch in). You need to cut a length of elastic that is just slightly shorter than the distance round your body here. This way the elastic will cling to your body.

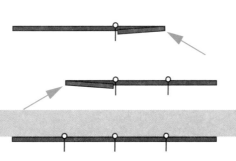

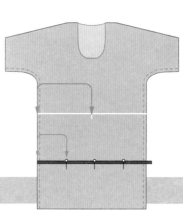

37_ Fold your elastic in half and put a pin in it at the centre point.

38_ Fold each end of your elastic in towards your central pin and put a pin in at the fold, so that your elastic has three pins stuck into it, dividing the strip into equal quarters.

39_ Each quarter of your elastic should be shorter than one-quarter of your dress.

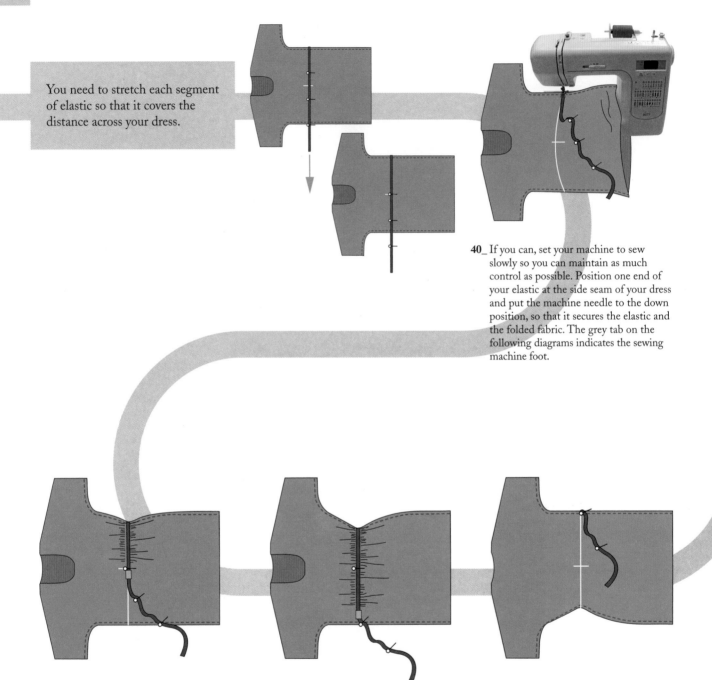

You need to stretch each segment of elastic so that it covers the distance across your dress.

40_ If you can, set your machine to sew slowly so you can maintain as much control as possible. Position one end of your elastic at the side seam of your dress and put the machine needle to the down position, so that it secures the elastic and the folded fabric. The grey tab on the following diagrams indicates the sewing machine foot.

41_ Hold the far end of the elastic with your left hand, and with your right hand pull your elastic so that your first pin reaches the central mark on the front of your dress. You need to sew your elastic into this position. Sew slowly and keep the elastic stretched as you go, holding it with both hands and letting the machine feed the fabric and the elastic through.

42_ When you get to the central mark, hold the elastic at the second pin with your right hand and pull it until it reaches the side seam of your dress. Sew this section of elastic down.

43_ When you reach the side seam, rearrange your dress; swivel it around so you can see the whole of the back side.

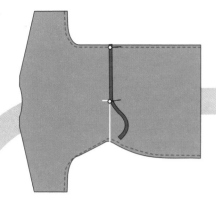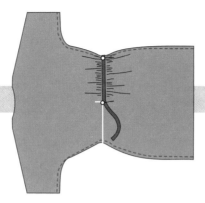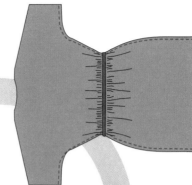

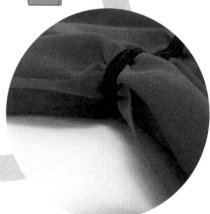

44_ Pull the elastic again so that the third pin reaches the central mark on the back of your dress and sew this part down.

45_ Finally, pull the end of your elastic until it reaches all the way back to where you began. Sew this last section of elastic down.

If you are using a wide piece of elastic, sew one edge of your elastic into place in the same way as you would sew a narrow piece of elastic. With the first edge secure, position your needle over the second edge and put the needle in the down position so that it is going through your elastic. Stretch out your dress and the elastic, pulling them towards you so that they have no wrinkles, and sew slowly along this edge until you get back to where you started.

You need to finish the curved neck edge of your dress with bias binding. See page 14 for guidance on this. Finally, you need to finish the bottom of your dress and your sleeve endings. You can hem them, or finish them with bias binding for decoration.

*you have made
a grecian dress*

ZIP

WAISTBAND   BACK   FRONT

03.

the skater skirt

The skater skirt is a circular skirt that hangs in folds. It is made using two half-circle pieces of fabric and one long rectangular strip of fabric to form the waistband. It fastens with a zip at the back, front or side.

TECHNICAL VARIATIONS

the skater skirt can be made and worn in a variety of ways

1_ ACID CANDY

2_ MONOCHROME ART

3_ AMERICAN ROAD TRIP

4_ RUDE DISCO

5_ COFFEE CLASSIC

6_ JUNGLE PUNK

7_ SAFARI PREP

8_ TEA PICNIC

1_ ACID CANDY

The Acid Candy skater skirt is made with a fairly stiff but thin pale blue polycotton. The initial measurement made along the fabric is 56cm (22in), creating a playful skirt that hangs mid-thigh. The completed waistband is 5cm (2in) deep. The zip sits at the side. The bottom edge of the skirt is finished with a shop-bought bias binding that matches the colour of the fabric.

2_ MONOCHROME ART

The Monochrome Art skater skirt is made using a very heavy, floppy fabric that has a stretch to it. The skirt falls with its own weight into multiple folds. The initial measurement made is 74cm (29in), and the skirt hangs well below the knees. The skirt fastens with a zip at the back. The front of the skirt is trimmed slightly so the skirt appears slightly longer at the sides than at the front. This skirt has a slim 4cm (1½in)-deep waistband and is finished at the bottom edge with a thin white bias binding.

3_ AMERICAN ROAD TRIP

The American Road Trip skater skirt is made using heavy, floppy mock velvet. The initial measurement made along the fabric is 56cm (22in). Each side of the skirt is then drawn and cut out as a rectangle, rather than a semi-circle, as shown. This creates corners that hang down in long, draping points. The waistband of this skirt is 4cm (1½in) deep and is much longer than the waist edge, extending beyond the zip on both sides. The extra lengths of material fasten in a bow at the back.

4_ RUDE DISCO

One side of the Rude Disco skater skirt is made using a stiff magenta fabric woven from metallic thread; the other is made of a fairly thick navy satin. The initial measurement is 46cm (18in), creating a short, party-time skirt that sticks out due to the stiffness of the fabrics. The waistband is a thick black satin and is an extremely deep 13.5cm (5¼in). The zip fastening sits at the centre front. The waistband is extended well beyond the zip area at both sides so that the ends can be tied together in a bow at the front (like the back of the American Road Trip skirt). The skirt is finished with black bias binding.

5_ COFFEE CLASSIC

The Coffee Classic skater skirt is made in a medium-weight, slightly stiff, black denim. The initial length measurement is 64cm (25in), creating a knee-length skirt that hangs in large undulating folds produced by the stiffness of the fabric. The skirt has a very deep 8cm (3¼in) waistband and fastens at the side. It is finished at the bottom with black bias binding.

6_ JUNGLE PUNK

The Jungle Punk skater skirt is made from a thin orange polycotton. It is made using five (rather than two) semi-circles of fabric, each one sloping from a longer vertical edge to a shallower vertical edge. Each time one piece is cut the centre is marked with a pin; then it is trimmed to make it shallower at one end. The skirt is then measured from the central pin to the shallower bottom end and a new semi-circle with this radius is drawn. The skirt wraps round and round over itself, creating a layered effect. It is finished with a contrasting black bias binding.

7_ SAFARI PREP

The Safari Prep skater skirt is made from a thin, extremely floppy patterned fabric. The fabric hangs down in very small folds, which gives it a fairly conservative appearance despite its short length. The initial measurement made along the fabric is 42cm (16½in). The zip fastening sits to one side. The skirt has a 5cm (2in)-deep waistband. It has been finished with red bias binding.

8_ TEA PICNIC

The Tea Picnic skater skirt is made using a light gingham print polycotton. The zip sits at the centre back of the skirt. The initial measurement made for the skirt length is 60cm (23½in). Once the pieces are cut and sewn together, the skirt is folded in half and trimmed at the front (see diagrams opposite) so the front of the skirt rises up, giving the skirt an extra-flouncy look. The skirt has a 6.5cm (2½in)-deep waistband. It is finished with a thick navy blue bias binding.

Measure how long you want the skirt to be by holding a tape measure at your waist and letting it hang down. Look in the mirror and see where you want the skirt to end. We'll call this your **length measurement**.

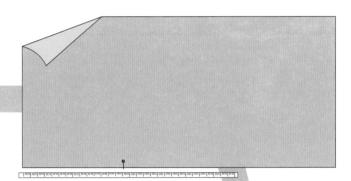

1_ Measure that distance horizontally across the bottom edge of your fabric and put a pin in here. We'll call this your **length pin**.

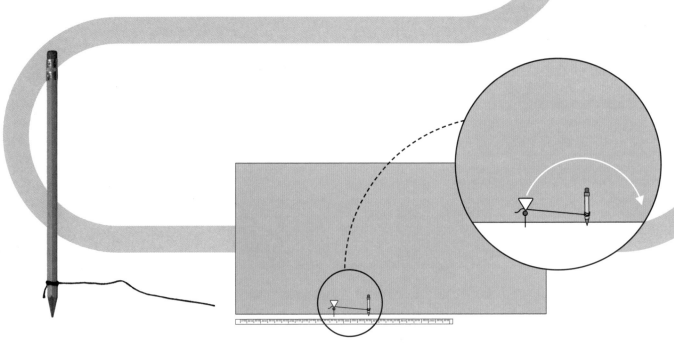

2_ Tie a piece of string to a pencil and cut it a few centimetres longer than your waist radius (see next step).

3_ You are going to draw a half-circle that will form the waist edge of your skirt. To get the correct measurement, measure the full distance around your waist or wherever you want your skirt to sit. Now, turn to a calculator and divide that number by 3.14 – the mysterious and miraculous pi! Finally, divide that number by two. We'll call this your **waist radius**.

4_ Hold your chalk, and the loose end of your string, together at your length pin. With the string held straight and tight, dig the pencil point in, continuing the horizontal line as shown.

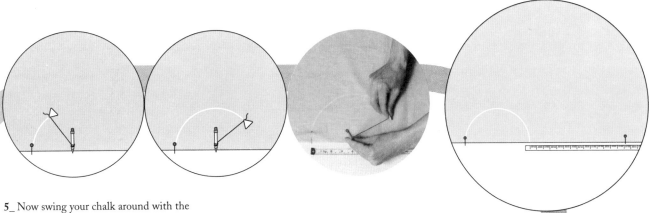

5_ Now swing your chalk around with the string, drawing a semi-circle.

6_ Measure your length measurement outwards from your semi-circle and put a pin in here.

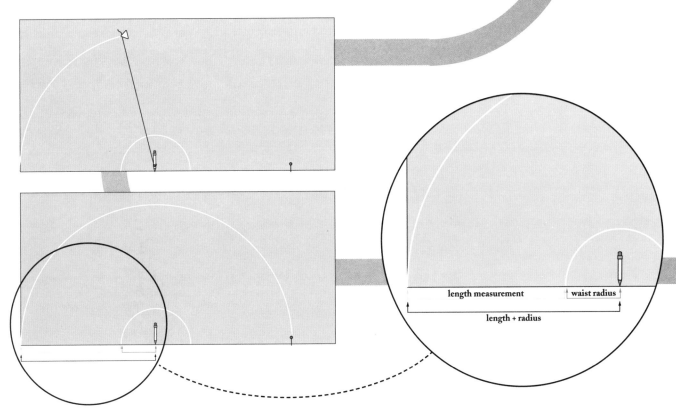

length measurement · waist radius

length + radius

7_ Now cut a piece of string that is as long as your length measurement plus your waist radius. (This is marked 'length+radius' with the black arrows on the diagram.)

8_ Hold your pencil in the same position and swing your chalk around again, drawing a large semi-circle that encases your little one. Cut along the lines of both your semi-circles. This piece makes up half of your skater skirt.

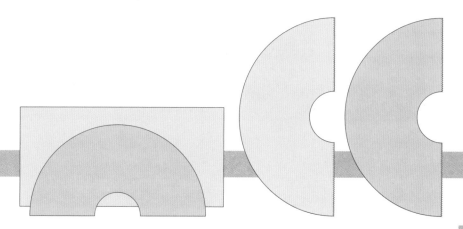

9_ Use this half to cut a second half that is exactly the same.

10_ Zigzag-stitch down all four straight edges – two on each piece.

Now you are going to join your two semi-circles to make one big circle.

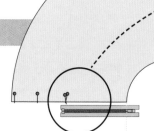

11_ Lay one of your halves out with the right side of the fabric facing upwards. Lay the second piece on top of it with the right side facing down.

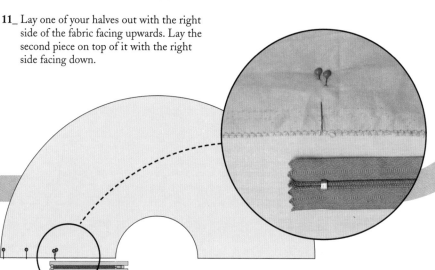

12_ Take your zip and lay it next to one of the straight edges with the pull tab at the centre of the semi-circle, which is where your waistband will be.

13_ The pull tab should sit above the edge (indicated by the yellow dotted line in the diagram). You need to join your semi-circles together with straight stitch just up to the point where the bottom of your zip sits.

14_ Pin along this stretch of fabric. Put two pins in level with the bottom of your zip, to remind yourself to stop sewing there.

The Jungle Punk skater skirt is a wraparound skirt that hangs in ever-shorter layers. You need to join more than two semi-circles of fabric to achieve this effect.

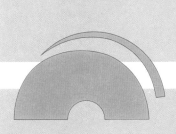 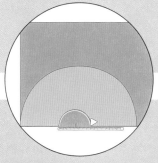 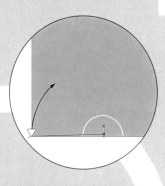

a_ Cut one semi-circle for your skirt. This will form the longest part of your skirt. Starting at one side, trim some fabric away, gradually moving closer to the original edge as you go.

b_ Now you have a piece that has a longer straight edge and a shorter straight edge. Flip the piece over and lay it out on your fabric with the shorter side meeting the edge of the fabric. Mark the waist circle with chalk, and use your tape measure to find the centre of your waist circle. Mark this with a pin.

c_ Using string, chalk and a pencil to pivot, draw a semi-circle onto your fabric. This will be as deep as the shorter straight edge of the trimmed piece, all the way round.

 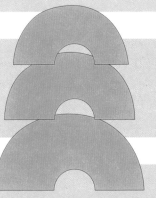 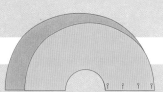 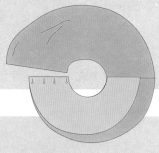

d_ Cut this piece out and again trim inwards from one side. Make sure it is the same side that you trimmed before (if you were looking at the right side of your fabric and trimmed the right-hand side, do the same this time too).

e_ Repeat these steps until you have as many pieces as you would like to use. Number them with chalk as you go, so you remember which piece is which.

f_ Lay your first, biggest piece out with the right side of the fabric facing up and lay the second piece on top of it with the right side facing down. Line up the two edges that match and pin them together, then sew all the way along this edge with a line of straight stitch.

g_ Open the joined pieces out and keep joining your pieces in this way until you have made a long spiral of pieces that gradually gets smaller and smaller. You can wrap this piece round and round your body to make the tiered effect. You will need to make an extra long waistband to cover the full top edge of your skirt. The easiest way to fasten this skirt is with a safety pin. You can also use a button, as long as you make sure there is a hole to push it through on every layer of your wrapped skirt.

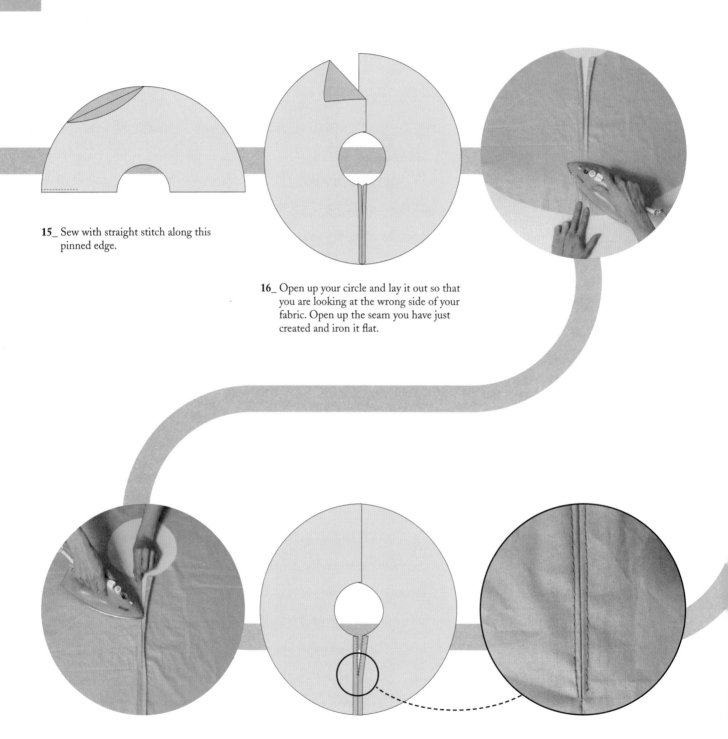

15_ Sew with straight stitch along this pinned edge.

16_ Open up your circle and lay it out so that you are looking at the wrong side of your fabric. Open up the seam you have just created and iron it flat.

17_ Continue ironing the flaps of fabric beyond the part you stitched to create two straight pressed edges.

18_ Neaten these ironed edges with a row of straight stitch running close to the edge.

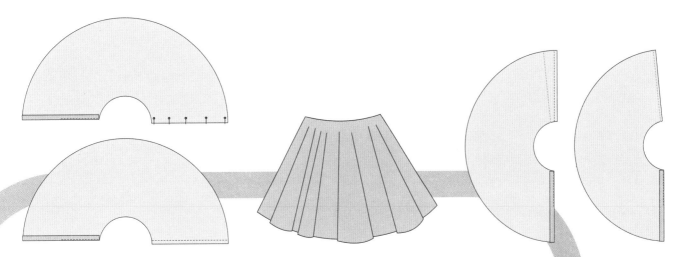

19_ Pin and sew along the second pair of straight edges and try the skirt on, holding your zip edges together so you get an idea of how the skirt fits.

Once your skirt is the right size at the waist, you need to cut a strip of fabric to make your waistband.

20_ If it is too small at the waist, trim some fabric away all the way around your waist circle. If it is too big, sew your lines of straight stitch further inland and trim away the excess fabric and the previous line of stitching. Then zigzag stitch over the new raw edges. This will slightly alter the way your skirt hangs, but you will hardly notice the difference and your skirt will fit.

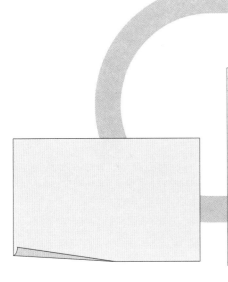

21_ Fold the edge of your fabric upwards.

22_ The flap you make needs to be as deep as you would like your waistband to be, plus an extra 3cm (1¼in) for hemming. Measure the flap.

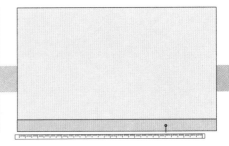

23_ The waistband needs to be about 8cm (3¼in) longer than the distance around the waist edge of your skirt. Measure this total distance along your fabric and put a pin in there. If you want to tie a bow at the waistband, as in the American Road Trip and Rude Disco skirts, allow extra fabric.

24_ Cut out your waistband piece and lay this strip out with the wrong side of the fabric facing upwards.

25_ Fold each short edge inwards about 1.5cm (⅝in) and iron it flat. Then stitch it down with a row of straight stitch running close to the edge.

26_ Iron a 1.5cm (⅝in) hem along each long edge, then fold the whole strip in half lengthways and iron it.

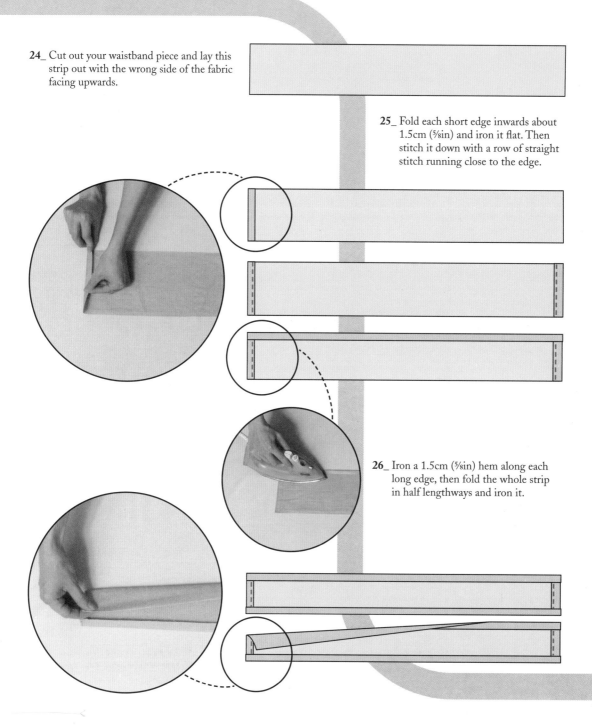

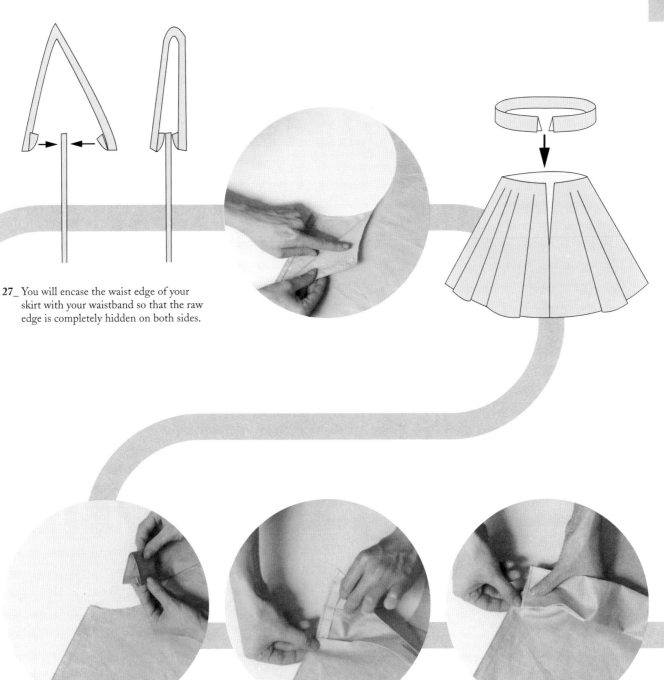

27_ You will encase the waist edge of your skirt with your waistband so that the raw edge is completely hidden on both sides.

28_ Start by lining up one of your short waistband edges with the neat zip edge.

29_ Put a pin in so that it goes through the front of your waistband, your skirt, and the back of your waistband.

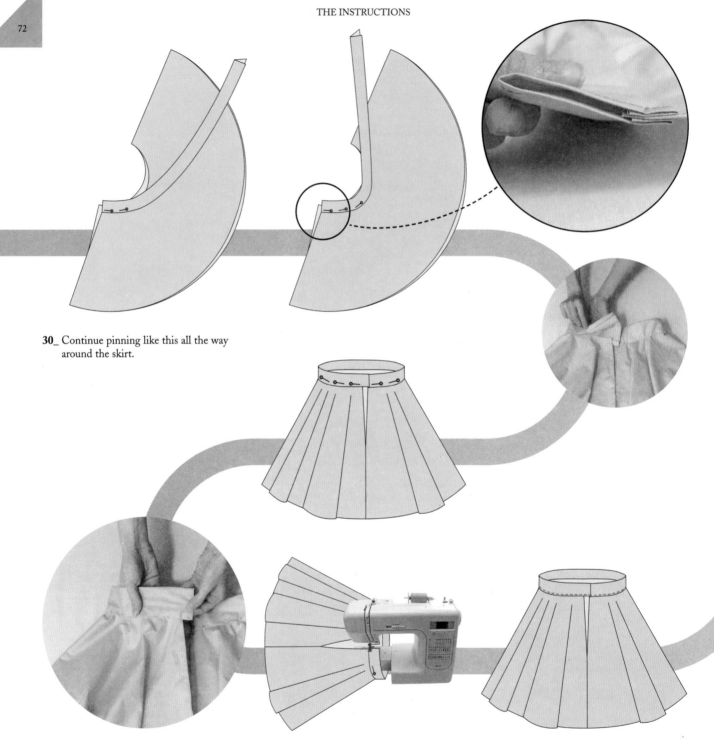

30_ Continue pinning like this all the way around the skirt.

31_ You should be left with a flap of waistband that is longer than your skirt. Pin the front of your waistband directly to the back here.

32_ With your waistband completely pinned, sew roughly over the pinned edge with large hand-stitches and remove your pins. If you are too impatient for this, you can dive straight into sewing, but the pins may prick you a few times. You now need to sew the waistband to the skirt with straight stitch, making sure your stitches catch both edges of your waistband and your skirt, sandwiched in the middle. Remove your hand-stitches with your quick unpick tool.

Now you need to sew your zip
into the space you have left for it.

33_ Slip the zip into position behind the
gap you left for it, so that the zipper sits
behind the waistband.

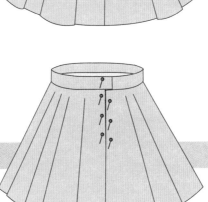

34_ Pin your zip into position with the neat
edge of your fabric sitting over the central
line that runs down your zip. The zip
should be pretty much covered by fabric.

35_ Turn your skirt inside out, so you can
clearly see your zip.

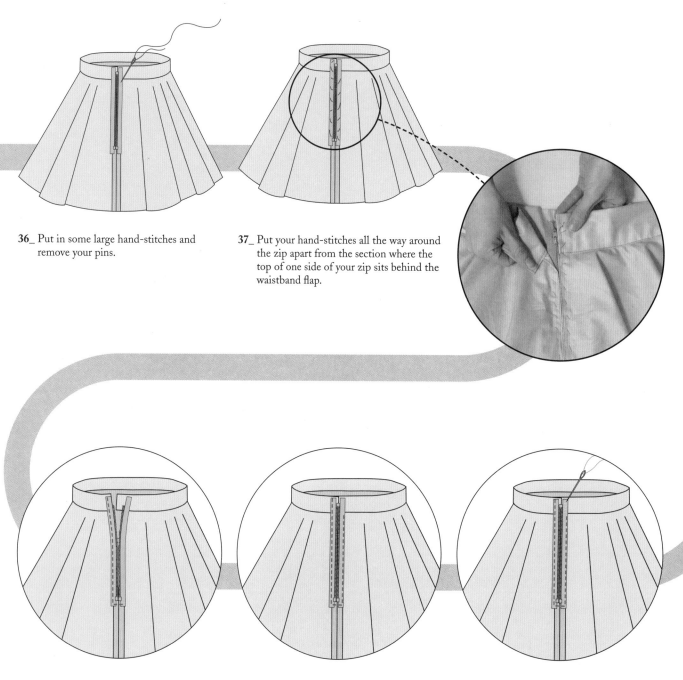

36_ Put in some large hand-stitches and remove your pins.

37_ Put your hand-stitches all the way around the zip apart from the section where the top of one side of your zip sits behind the waistband flap.

38_ You are now going to sew this with your machine. Sew all the way around your zip with straight stitch, leaving the last, unattached section unsewn.

39_ With a needle and thread, finish sewing your zip to your waistband. You can just catch the fabric so that your stitches won't appear on the right side of your waistband.

40_ Finish the bottom edge of your skirt with bias binding (see page 14 for guidance on this). Finally, finish your waistband with a popper or button.

you have made a skater skirt

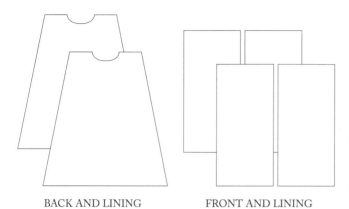

BACK AND LINING   FRONT AND LINING

04.

the waistcoat

The waistcoat is made up of a flared back piece with a shaped neckline and two rectangular front pieces. It is lined with three identical lining pieces. The corners of the front pieces fold down to form a collar, so you can use the lining to show a contrasting fabric or colour.

TECHNICAL VARIATIONS

the waistcoat can be made and worn in a variety of ways

1_ ACID CANDY

2_ MONOCHROME ART

3_ AMERICAN ROAD TRIP

4_ RUDE DISCO

5_ COFFEE CLASSIC

6_ JUNGLE PUNK

7_ SAFARI PREP

8_ TEA PICNIC

1_ ACID CANDY

The Acid Candy waistcoat is made using quite a tough, medium-weight fabric with a rough, visible weave. It is lined with a thin polycotton. The pieces have been cut 62cm (24½in) deep. The two front pieces are 28cm (11in) wide and are attached to the back to form a fairly wide shoulder seam of 10cm (4in). This gives the appearance of almost squared, power shoulders. All the other waistcoats have narrower shoulders. The waistcoat has a belt loop on either side at the front and one at the back.

2_ MONOCHROME ART

The Monochrome Art waistcoat is made with black polycotton on the outside and lined with white polycotton, to give it a smart, dinner-jacket feel. It is made using the same dimensions as the Acid Candy waistcoat. Each lapel is ironed to fold down at a different angle to give the waistcoat an asymmetric appearance. The waistcoat is worn with a wide belt that does not require belt loops.

3_ AMERICAN ROAD TRIP

The American Road Trip waistcoat is made using a stiff denim and is lined with a velveteen fabric. It is cropped so that it hangs just above the waist – the pieces are cut 39cm (15½in) deep. The two front pieces are 28cm (11in) wide. This waistcoat is hand-sewn at the front and sides, but is wide enough to slip on over the head.

4_ RUDE DISCO

The Rude Disco waistcoat is made with a thick black satin and a thick magenta fabric woven from metallic threads. The magenta is used as a lining on one of the front pieces and as the outer fabric on the second front piece. All the pieces are cut at a fairly short 48cm (19in) deep, while the front pieces measure 34cm (13½in) across. A square is cut away from one corner of each of the front pieces before the lining and outers are sewn together. This is a very simple way of creating a shaped lapel. The waistcoat has no belt loops and is instead sewn together at each side and worn with the front open.

5_ COFFEE CLASSIC

The Coffee Classic waistcoat is made using a floppy crêpe-like fabric and is lined with brushed cotton. The pieces are cut 61cm (24in) deep. The two front pieces are 28cm (11in) wide. Each shoulder measures a slim 5cm (2in) across, so this waistcoat has a more lady-like feel than the masculine Acid Candy waistcoat, revealing bare shoulders. The lapels are shaped in the same way as the Rude Disco waistcoat. The waistcoat has a belt loop on either side at the front and one at the back, and is worn with a thick belt.

6_ JUNGLE PUNK

The Jungle Punk waistcoat is made with a thin black polycotton on the outside and a contrasting tangerine polycotton on the inside. All the pieces are cut 54cm (21¼in) deep. The two front pieces are fairly narrow at 24cm (9½in) wide, making slim lapels. A long, slim rectangle is cut away from one corner of each of the front pieces to create a shaped lapel. The waistcoat has elegant slim shoulder seams measuring an extremely narrow 4cm (1½in), and no belt loops. The two front pieces are hand-sewn together and a popper or press-stud is added at each side to fasten the back and front pieces.

7_ SAFARI PREP

The Safari Prep waistcoat is the longest waistcoat. All the pieces are cut 67cm (26½in) deep. The waistcoat is made from a tough printed cotton and is lined with maroon suiting. The front pieces are 26cm (10¼in) wide and meet the back piece with a fairly slim 5cm (2in) shoulder seam. The lapels of this waistcoat are folded once, then the corner of that fold is tucked under again to create a more gradual angle. These folds are ironed into place. The waistcoat has a belt loop on both sides at the front and one central loop at the back.

8_ TEA PICNIC

The Tea Picnic waistcoat is made with thin flowery printed polycotton on the outside and plain white polycotton on the inside. The pieces are cut quite long, at 66cm (26in) deep, while the front pieces measure 36cm (14in) across. One corner of each front piece is trimmed off at a curve before the lining and outer pieces are sewn together, to create gently rounded lapels. The waistcoat has one belt loop at the front and three across the back. It is worn with a thin belt.

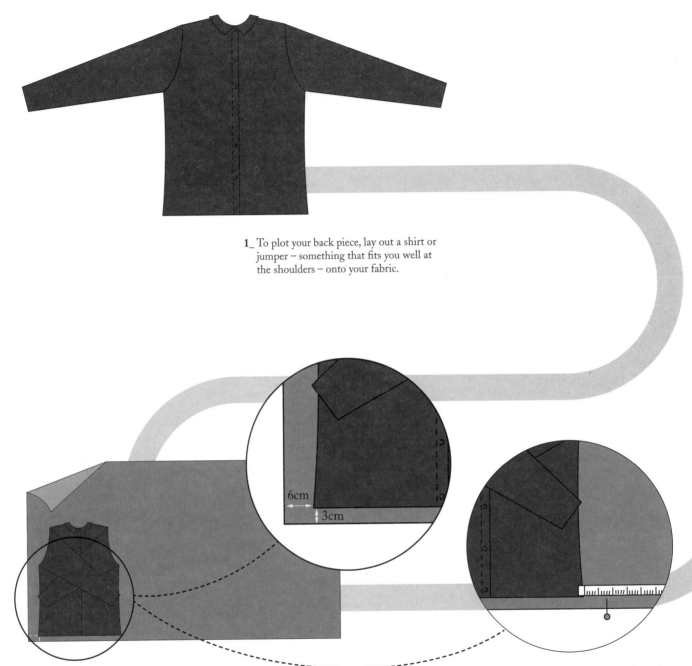

1_ To plot your back piece, lay out a shirt or jumper – something that fits you well at the shoulders – onto your fabric.

6cm

3cm

2_ Lay your shirt about 6cm (2½in) inland from the side of your fabric. This creates a flare. You can choose to make your flare wider. If you want your waistcoat to be the same length as your shirt, lay the shirt about 3cm (1¼in) up from the bottom of your fabric, to allow for making seams. You can make your waistcoat much longer or shorter than your shirt (see the variations on pages 78–79).

3_ Measure 6cm (2½in) across from the right side of your shirt so that you add the same amount of extra width at both sides. Put a pin in here.

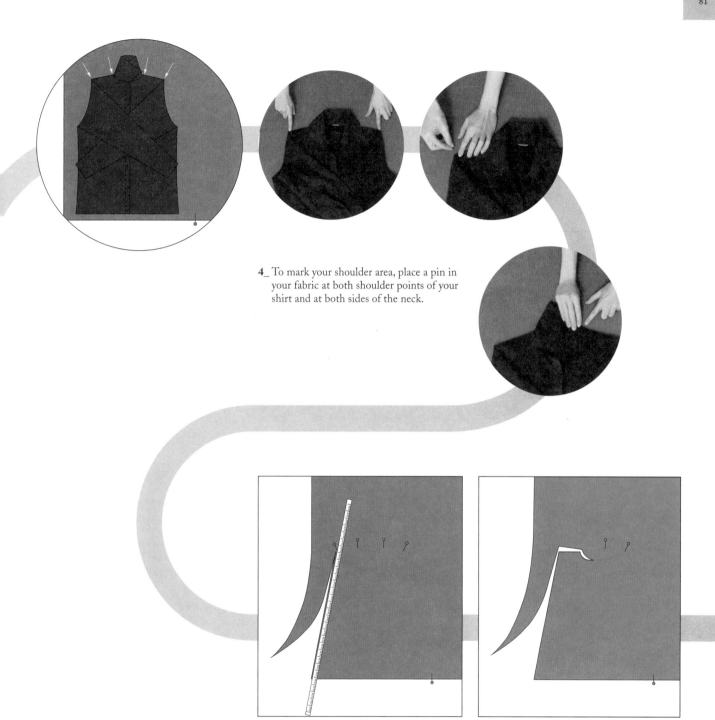

4_ To mark your shoulder area, place a pin in your fabric at both shoulder points of your shirt and at both sides of the neck.

5_ Remove your shirt and cut a sloping line upwards from the bottom left corner of your fabric to the left shoulder pin.

6_ You can make the next cut freestyle or use a sheet of newspaper or your tape measure to guide you. Cut horizontally across from the left shoulder pin to the neck pin. Now cut a curved line dipping down to form half a neckline.

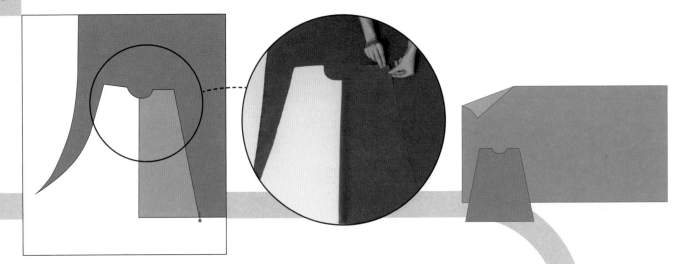

7_ Take hold of the flap you have cut and fold it over to the right. Use your right shoulder pin and right bottom pin to settle the flap into the accurate position on your fabric.

8_ Now use your folded first half as a guide to cut your second half exactly the same. You have now made your back piece.

9_ Take your back piece and use it as a guide to cut a piece from your lining fabric that is exactly the same shape.

Next you are going to cut your two front pieces. Each piece is a rectangle. Each rectangle will be the same height as your back piece, and as wide as half the bottom width of your back piece.

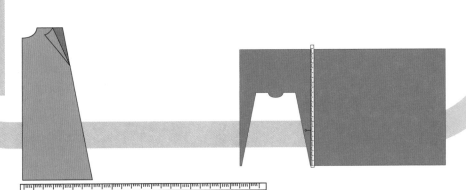

10_ Fold your back piece in half vertically and measure the distance across the bottom.

11_ Measure that distance up from the bottom of your fabric and put a pin in to mark the place. Cut upwards from the bottom of your fabric to the pin.

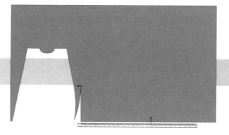

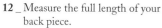

13 _ Measure this distance across the bottom
of your fabric and put a pin in to mark
that spot.

12 _ Measure the full length of your
back piece.

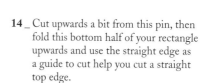

14 _ Cut upwards a bit from this pin, then
fold this bottom half of your rectangle
upwards and use the straight edge as
a guide to cut help you cut a straight
top edge.

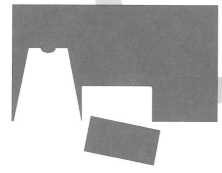

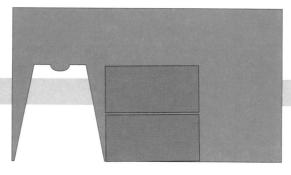

15_ This is your first front piece. Use your
first front rectangle as a guide to cut your
second one exactly the same.

16_ Lay these shapes out onto your lining
fabric and cut two front lining pieces
exactly the same.

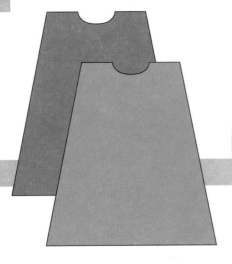

17_ Now you are going to join your outer back piece to your lining piece. Lay your outer piece out with the right side of the fabric facing upwards and lay your lining piece on top of it with the right side facing down.

18_ You should be looking at the wrong side of your lining fabric.

19_ Pin the two pieces together at the neckline, down each side and across the bottom. You need to sew the two together with straight stitch, leaving a gap of about 10cm (4in) at the bottom.

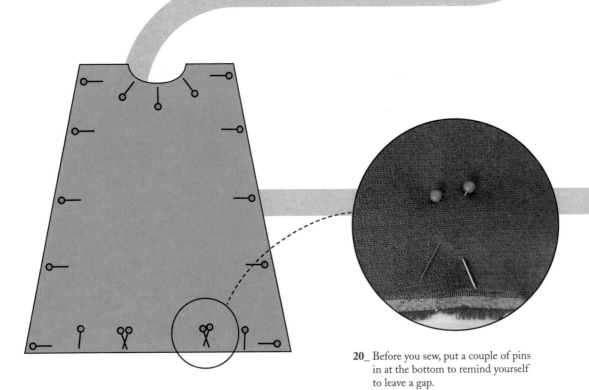

20_ Before you sew, put a couple of pins in at the bottom to remind yourself to leave a gap.

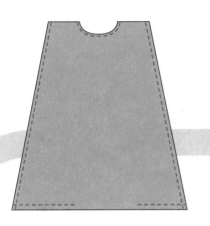

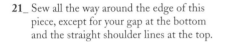

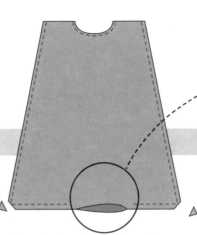

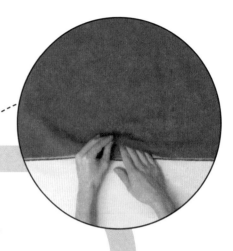

21_ Sew all the way around the edge of this piece, except for your gap at the bottom and the straight shoulder lines at the top.

22_ Trim the bottom two corners of your piece diagonally so this seam fabric doesn't bunch up into a lump when you turn your piece the right way out.

23_ Put your hand into the gap you have left, take hold of the fabric, and pull the inside out, so that you are looking at the right side of your lining fabric and the right side of your outer fabric.

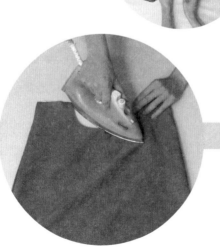

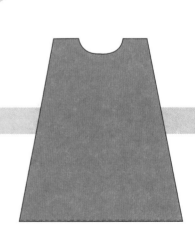

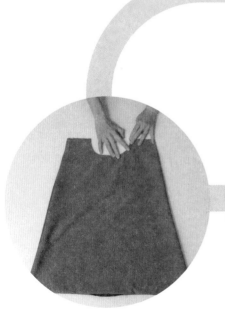

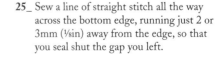

24_ Flatten the piece, pulling at the seams with your fingertips, and iron it so that the lining and outer fabric sit neatly together.

25_ Sew a line of straight stitch all the way across the bottom edge, running just 2 or 3mm (⅛in) away from the edge, so that you seal shut the gap you left.

You can shape your front pieces to produce a different shape of collar. The waistcoats with shaped lapels all began with rectangular front pieces that were trimmed to create a different shape. The Jungle Punk front pieces have had rectangles cut out at one corner to make double lapels. The Tea Picnic front pieces have had one corner trimmed into a curve.

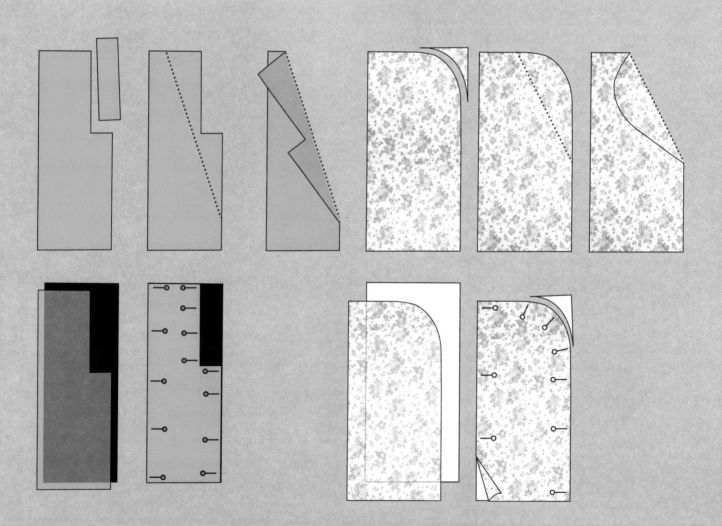

Now you need to join the lining and the outer of your front rectangles in the same way.

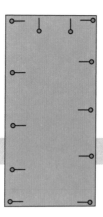 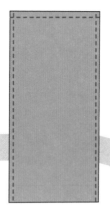 

26_ Rather than leaving a gap, leave one complete short end unsewn.

27_ Trim the corners of your rectangle, then turn it the right way around.

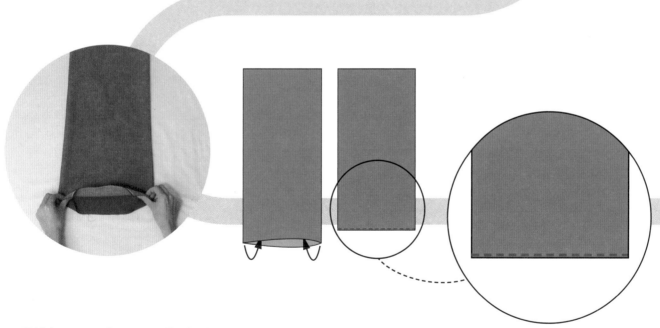

28_ Fold the unsewn edge in on itself and seal it with a line of straight stitch running close to the edge.

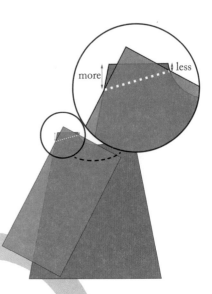

Now you have a complete back piece and two complete front pieces. Next, you need to join them together at the shoulder.

29_ Lay your back piece out so that you are looking at your outer fabric. Take your first front rectangle and lay it on top of your back piece, right side down. Your front piece needs to sit diagonally, with one corner matching up with the shoulder area of your back piece.

30_ You will sew the pieces together here with a line of straight stitch that needs to slope gradually upwards from the outer edge of the shoulder. Your front piece needs to be positioned so there is more fabric showing from the back piece on the outer part of the shoulder than there is on the inner part.

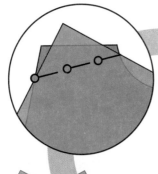

31_ Pin the two pieces together.

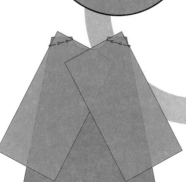

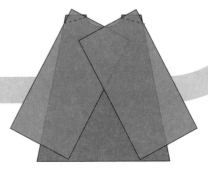

32_ Lay your second front piece out in the same way and pin.

33_ Put a few long hand-stitches in along your line of pins and remove the pins. Try on your waistcoat, folding the corners of your front rectangles down, to see if you are happy with the way it will sit.

34_ Adjust your front pieces accordingly, then sew them to your back piece at the shoulders with straight stitch.

35_ Trim the excess fabric and zigzag the flaps together. Push each zigzagged flap to one side and sew it flat with a line of straight stitch, as detailed in the Grecian dress instructions on page 56.

36_ Turn your waistcoat the right way out.

37_ Fold the front corners of your front pieces down to create lapels, and iron into place.

You can create belt loops for your waistcoat and use a belt to bring it in at the waist (see page 18 for guidance on this).

*you have made
a waistcoat*

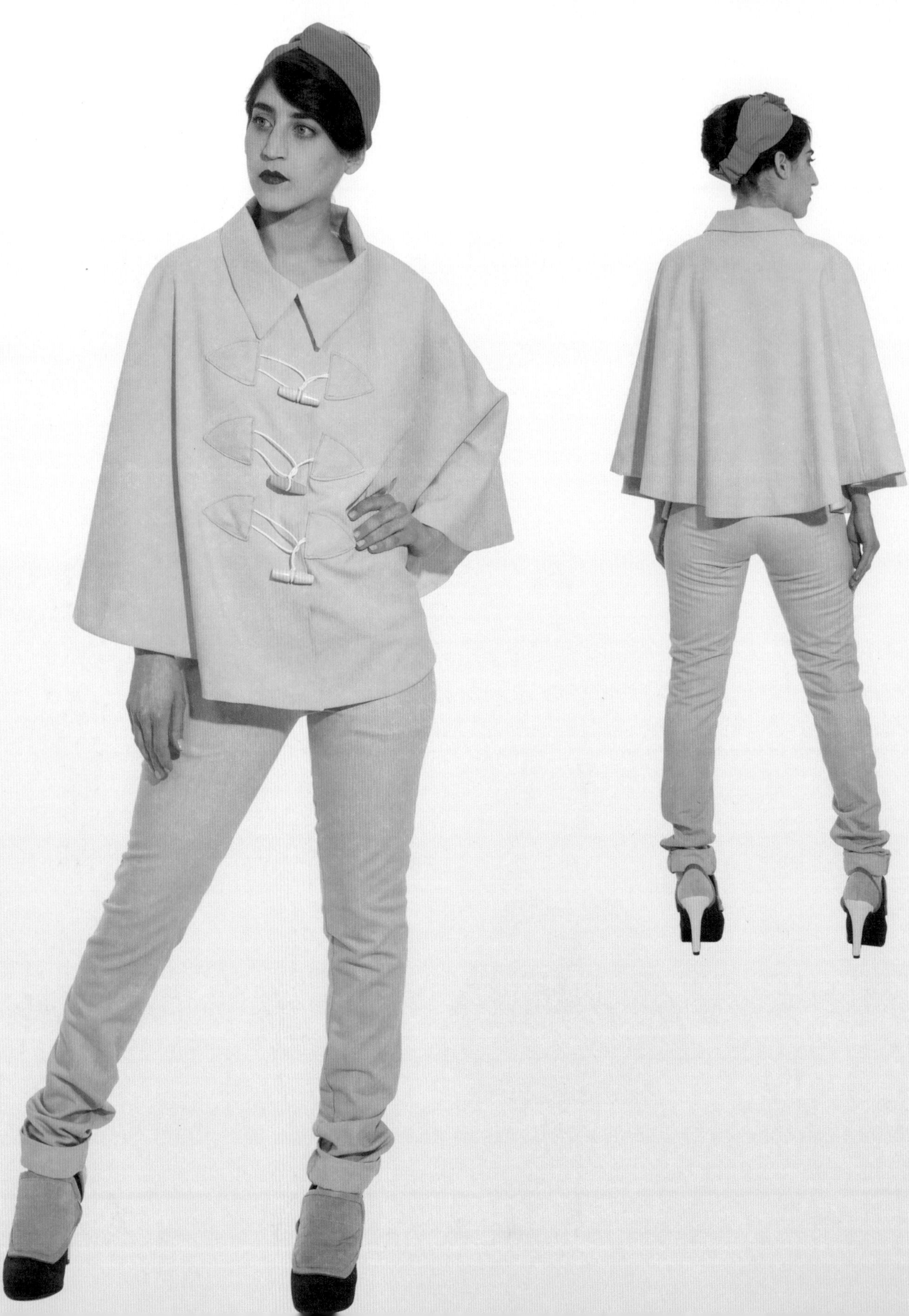

MAIN PIECES AND LINING

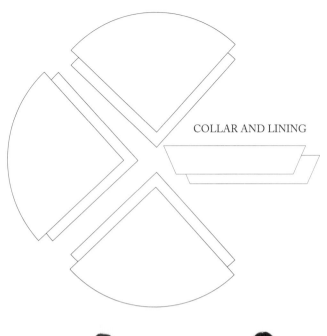

COLLAR AND LINING

05.

the cloak

The cloak is a lined cape that can be made to incorporate a hood or a collar. It can be fastened with buttons, Velcro, a zip or tie. The cloak is made up of three main quarter-circles of fabric like slices of pizza, with three identical pieces made of lining fabric. One long strip of fabric makes up the collar, with an identical lining piece.

TECHNICAL VARIATIONS

the cloak can be made and worn in a variety of ways

1_ ACID CANDY

2_ MONOCHROME ART

3_ AMERICAN ROAD TRIP

4_ RUDE DISCO

5_ COFFEE CLASSIC

6_ JUNGLE PUNK

7_ SAFARI PREP

8_ TEA PICNIC

1_ ACID CANDY

The Acid Candy cloak is made using a medium-weight fabric that hangs quite stiffly and is lined with a thin polycotton. It has quite a deep 10.5cm (4⅛in) collar that has been pinched together at the front with a hook and eye. The cloak is fastened with a duffle-style fastening using coloured elastic and sewn fabric patches. For guidance on making this, see the DIYcouture website (www.diy-couture.co.uk).

2_ MONOCHROME ART

The Monochrome Art cloak is made using an airy medium-weight woollen suiting and is lined using a heavy, floppy synthetic fabric, which gives the cloak its weight. The cloak pieces are cut at 91cm (36in), making an extremely long dress-like cloak that hangs below the wrist. Because of this, a few stitches are added to create a sleeve-like opening that can be pushed up above the wrist. The cloak is fastened with buttons and has a neat, pointy 6cm (2½in)-deep collar made of thin black polycotton.

3_ AMERICAN ROAD TRIP

The American Road Trip cloak is made using a thick woollen tweed, giving it a cosy, autumnal feel. It is lined with a medium-weight brushed cotton that is extremely floppy. The cloak is the same length as the Acid Candy cloak, but has an even deeper 14cm (5½in) collar. The cloak is fastened with strips of fabric that are made in exactly the same way as belt loops (see page 18). The strips are shaped into curved points and are tied together in knots.

4_ RUDE DISCO

The Rude Disco cloak is made with a shiny lamé fabric and lined with thin, floppy polyester. The cloak pieces are cut 51cm (20in) deep to make a fairly short cape. The cloak has a hood made using the instructions provided for the hoody (see pages 157–161), and attached in exactly the same way as the collar. The cloak is fastened with Velcro but has decorative buttons.

5_ COFFEE CLASSIC

The Coffee Classic cloak is made from a floppy crêpe-effect fabric in a neutral colour and lined with a heavy-weight brushed cotton. It is made using four – rather than three – quarter-circles of fabric, which causes more folds to form as the cloak drapes from the shoulders. The cloak has a 7cm (2¾in)-deep collar and fastens with a single button at the top of the front opening.

6_ JUNGLE PUNK

The Jungle Punk cloak is made from a fairly tough royal blue suiting fabric and lined with a thin but heavy green fabric. It is the shortest of all the cloak variations, the initial pieces measuring 43cm (17in) across. It is also the simplest cloak, with no hood or collar and a straightforward zip fastening.

7_ SAFARI PREP

The Safari Prep cloak is made using four rather than three quarter-circles of fabric. The central two are made of a stiff navy fabric and the outer two, which fall at the front, are made of a medium-weight burgundy suiting. The pieces are initially cut 54cm (21¼in) deep. The cloak is worn so that the navy blue pieces – which sit at the back – are visible at the shoulders and across the tops of the arms. The cloak has a pointed collar made from a single strip of fabric. Its edges are finished in contrasting cream bias binding. The front edges of the cloak overlap and are fastened with poppers that are not visible from the outside.

8_ TEA PICNIC

The Tea Picnic cloak is made from a floppy brushed cotton, but lined with a fairly stiff polycotton. The cloak pieces are cut just 46cm (18in) deep to make a cute, cropped cape. The cloak features a contrasting Peter Pan-style collar, with rounded ends. The collar is 6cm (2½in) deep and is made using just one layer of fabric that has been edged with bias binding. The cloak fastens with Velcro and has decorative heart-shaped buttons.

To begin, you need to cut your first shape. Hold the zero end of a tape measure at your shoulder and let it hang down. Decide how long you want your cloak. Add an extra 12cm (4¾in) to this and write the total down. We will call this your **length measurement.**

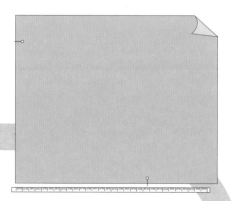

1_ Lay your fabric out and measure your length measurement along the vertical edge. Put a pin in to mark this point. Repeat this with the horizontal edge of your fabric. Your length measurement is now marked along two edges of your fabric.

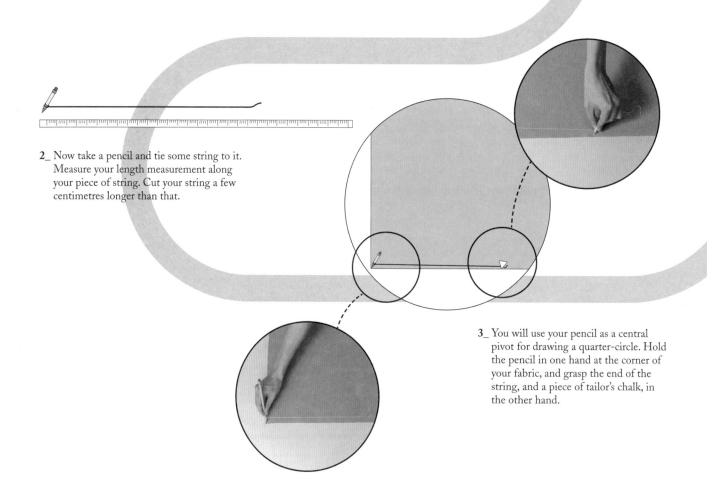

2_ Now take a pencil and tie some string to it. Measure your length measurement along your piece of string. Cut your string a few centimetres longer than that.

3_ You will use your pencil as a central pivot for drawing a quarter-circle. Hold the pencil in one hand at the corner of your fabric, and grasp the end of the string, and a piece of tailor's chalk, in the other hand.

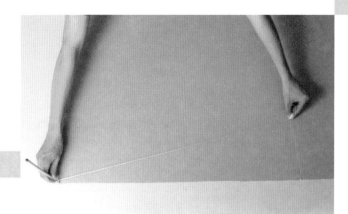

4_ Position your chalk at one of your pins and swing the string around, tracing the orbit you make with the chalk.

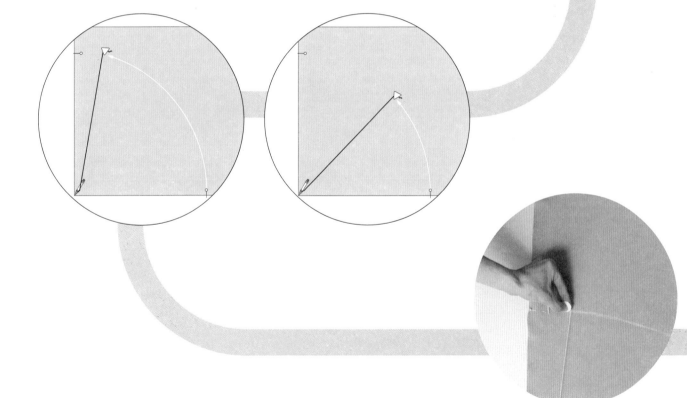

5_ Make your chalk circle finish at your second pin.

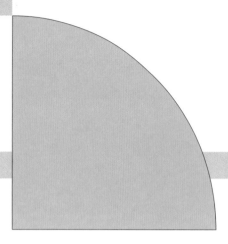

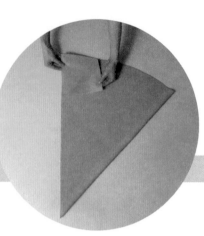

6_ Cut your chalk line, then fold your pizza-slice shape in half to check that it is symmetrical. If it is not, trim off any excess fabric along the curved edge.

You need to cut two more identical pieces from your main fabric. Use your first piece as a template and cut around it. Repeat this process so that you have three identical quarter-circles made of your main fabric.

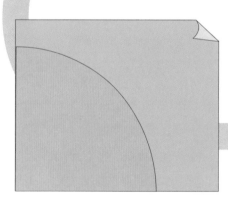

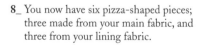

7_ You also need to cut three identical pieces from your lining fabric. Use one of your cut pieces as a guide to do this.

8_ You now have six pizza-shaped pieces; three made from your main fabric, and three from your lining fabric.

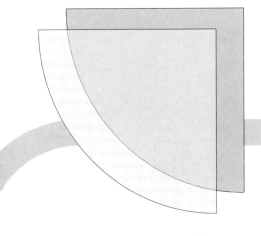

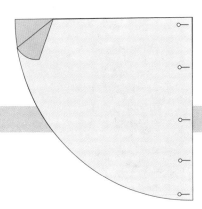

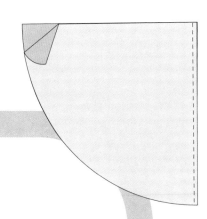

9_ Next you are going to join two of your main pieces of fabric together. Lay one of your pieces out flat with the right side of the fabric facing upwards. Take another piece and lay it directly on top of the first, with the right side of the fabric facing down.

10_ Pin the two pieces together along one of the straight edges.

11_ Sew along this edge with a line of straight stitch running about 1.5cm (⅝in) away from the edge.

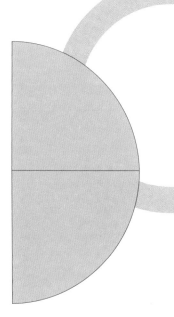

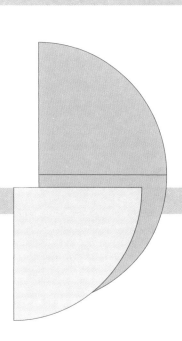

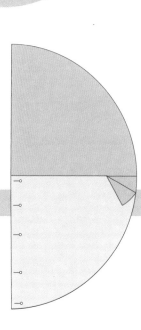

12_ Now you can join your third piece to these two. Fold the joined pieces out flat so you are looking at the right side of both of them, in the shape of a semi-circle.

13_ Lay your third, unattached piece on top of one of your joined pieces, with the right side of the fabric facing down.

14_ Your third piece will be slightly deeper than the one you are laying it on, as that piece has lost some fabric to a seam. Match your third piece up at the bottom, curved edge. Again, pin down the unjoined edge of the piece and sew the two together with straight stitch.

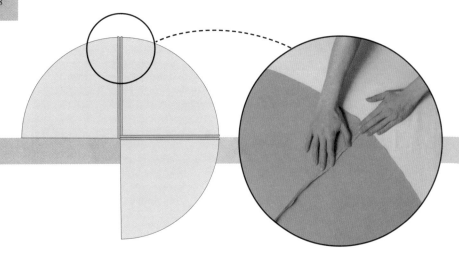

15_ Fold your whole piece out, with the wrong side of the fabric facing upwards. You will be looking at three-quarters of a circle. You will be able to see flaps of fabric where you have sewn your pieces together. Spread out the flaps of fabric along the joins, as if you are opening a book. If you are making a variation that uses four pieces of fabric, attach the fourth piece now.

16_ Iron the flaps firmly or with a bit of steam so that they sit flat.

17_ Repeat this joining process with your three pieces of lining fabric.

Now you need to attach the lining to the outer cloak piece to form a large cloak-shaped pocket.

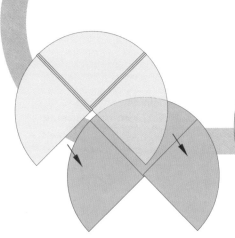

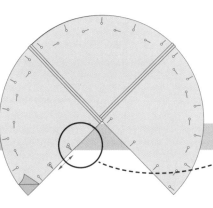

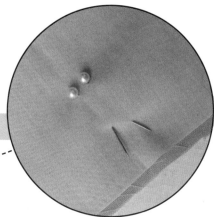

18_ Lay out your outer piece with the right side facing upwards. Lay the lining piece on top with the right side facing down.

19_ Pin the two pieces together all the way around the curved edge and the two straight edges. You need to leave a 10cm (4in) gap along one of the straight edges so that you can put your hand inside the cloak later.

20_ Stick a pair of pins in at either end of your planned gap to remind yourself to stop sewing.

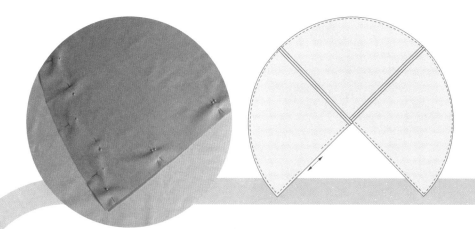

21_ If you have enough pins, you can add an extra row all the way around your cloak, pinned horizontally into your cloak. This will help keep your fabric stable as you are sewing.

22_ Sew with straight stitch all the way around your pinned edges, about 1cm (⅜in) away from the edge. Sew slowly, guiding the fabric with your hands spread flat. Remember to leave your 10cm (4in) gap unsewn.

Now you need to cut a space for your neck.

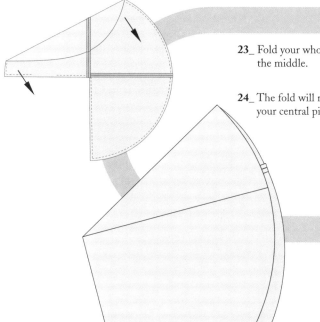

23_ Fold your whole cloak in half down the middle.

24_ The fold will run down the middle of your central pizza slice.

Now decide how large you would like your neck hole to be. The Acid Candy cloak shown here uses a measurement of 10cm (4in) along each straight edge. You can make the hole much wider – for example, if you want a large hood. See the variations on pages 92–93 to help you decide.

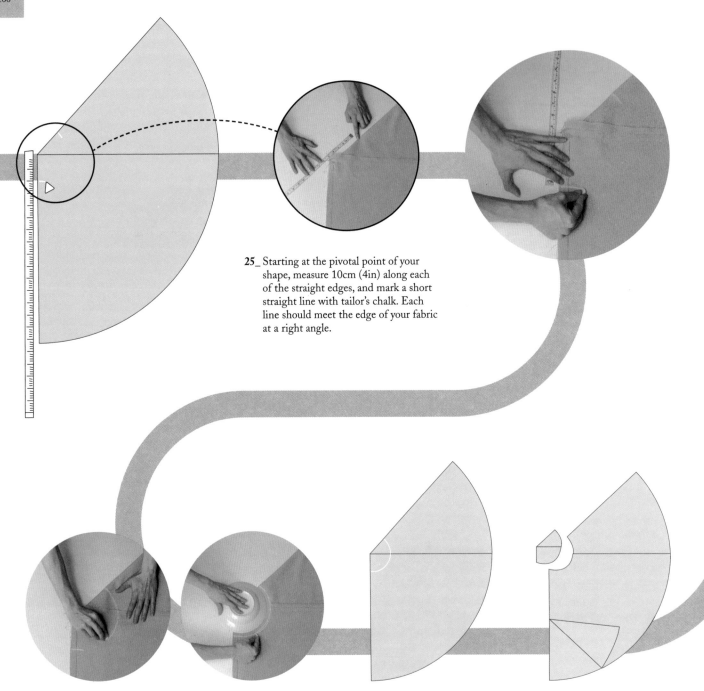

25_ Starting at the pivotal point of your shape, measure 10cm (4in) along each of the straight edges, and mark a short straight line with tailor's chalk. Each line should meet the edge of your fabric at a right angle.

26_ You need to join these two straight lines with a curved line. You can draw this freestyle, or you can use any circular object such as a small plate or a CD as a guide.

27_ Cut along your chalk line and open your cloak out.

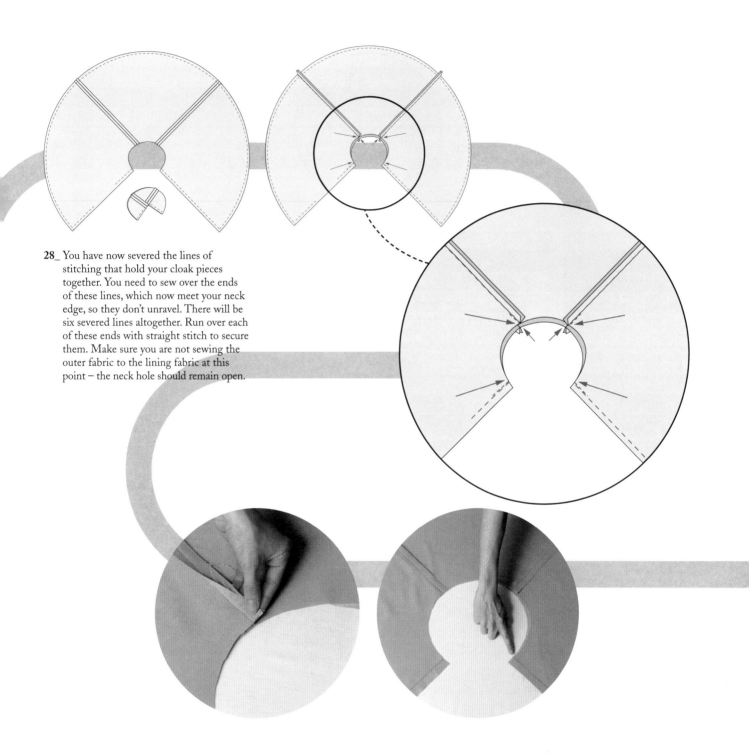

28_ You have now severed the lines of
stitching that hold your cloak pieces
together. You need to sew over the ends
of these lines, which now meet your neck
edge, so they don't unravel. There will be
six severed lines altogether. Run over each
of these ends with straight stitch to secure
them. Make sure you are not sewing the
outer fabric to the lining fabric at this
point – the neck hole should remain open.

Now make your collar.

If you want to make a hood, follow the instructions for the hoody on pages 157–161 and insert it in exactly the same way as the collar.

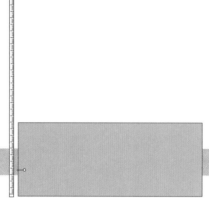

29_ Decide how deep you would like your collar to be. Look at the variations on pages 92–93 to help you decide. Add 3cm (1¼in) to the depth you want and measure this upwards from the bottom of your fabric. Put a pin in here. The collar shown here is 10.5cm (4⅛in) deep.

30_ Take some string or thread and cut a piece that is the same length as the distance around the neck edge of your cloak, shown by the pink arrow in the diagram.

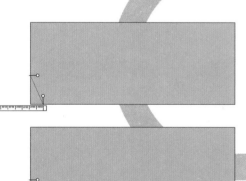

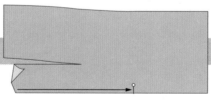

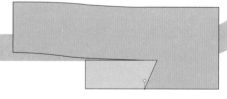

31_ Take this piece of string and lay it out on/under your fabric, along a straight edge. Lay the string slightly inland – about 6cm (2½in). This will allow you to cut a sloped end for your collar. Cut this sloped end now.

32_ Next, cut about halfway along the horizontal top edge of your planned collar piece and fold this cut half over.

33_ Use this folded half as a guide to cut your second half exactly the same.

34_ Use this piece to cut a lining piece exactly the same size. Pin the two pieces together with right sides touching each other.

35_ Sew these two pieces together along the longest long edge and down both sloping short sides.

36_ If you want your collar to have pointed ends, trim the pointed corners now.

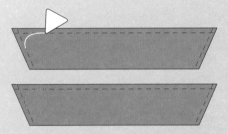

37_ If you would like a collar with rounded ends, like the Coffee Classic cloak, mark a curve onto one side of your collar piece with tailor's chalk, then sew along this line. If not, go on to step 40.

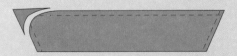

38_ Trim the fabric close to the sewn curve – about 3 or 4mm (³⁄₁₆in) away – then fold your collar in half again and use the curved side as a guide to mark the second curve.

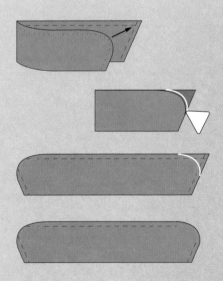

39_ Sew your second curve inside the line you have drawn and trim your second side.

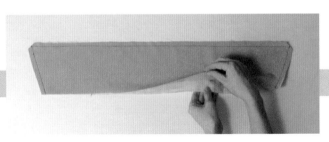

40_ Turn your collar the right way round.

41_ Iron it flat, so that all the sewn edges sit neatly. Poke your finger into the corners to get them as pointy as possible. If you have a knitting needle, poke it in to the corners to push the fabric out into a point. Sew a line of straight stitch along the bottom, unsewn edge of your collar just to keep those edges together.

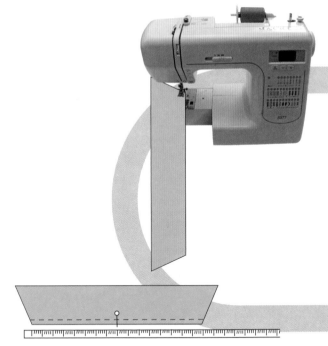

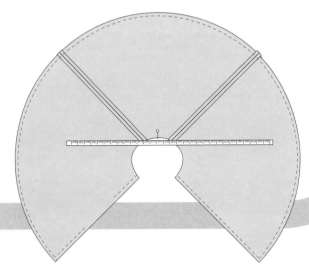

42_ Now find the centre of your collar by folding it in half, or by using your tape measure, and put a pin in there.

43_ Find the centre of the neck edge of your cloak and put pins in both the lining and outer fabrics there.

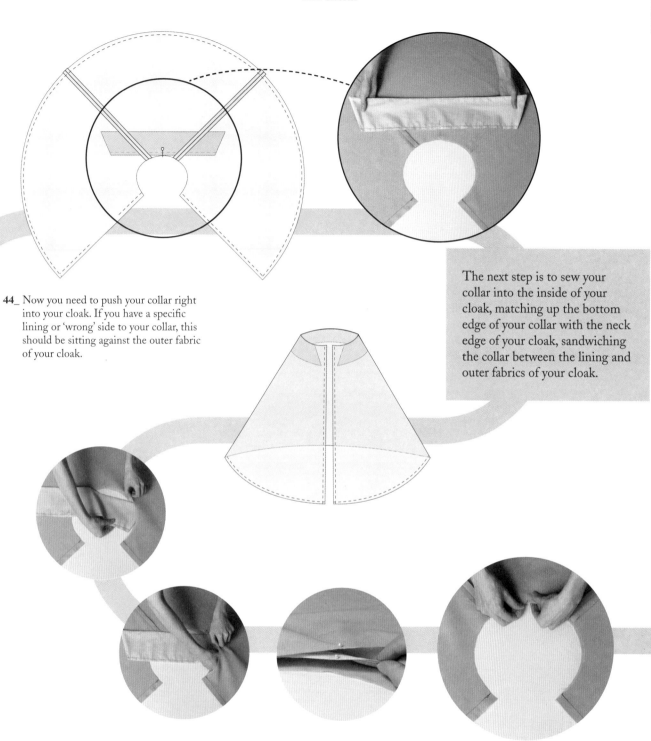

44_ Now you need to push your collar right into your cloak. If you have a specific lining or 'wrong' side to your collar, this should be sitting against the outer fabric of your cloak.

The next step is to sew your collar into the inside of your cloak, matching up the bottom edge of your collar with the neck edge of your cloak, sandwiching the collar between the lining and outer fabrics of your cloak.

45_ Line up the three centre pins – on the lining of your cloak, your collar, and the outer fabric of your cloak. Take out all three centre pins and replace them with one pin, which goes through all the layers of fabric.

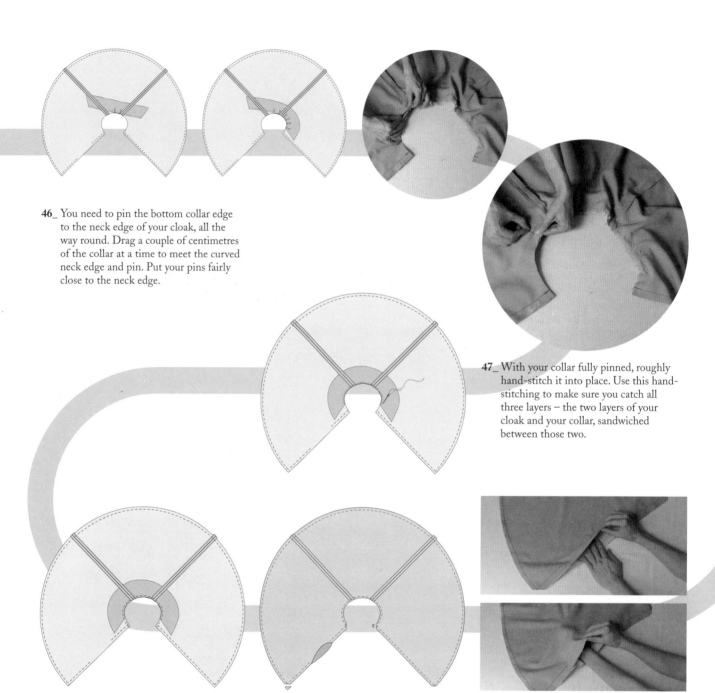

46_ You need to pin the bottom collar edge to the neck edge of your cloak, all the way round. Drag a couple of centimetres of the collar at a time to meet the curved neck edge and pin. Put your pins fairly close to the neck edge.

47_ With your collar fully pinned, roughly hand-stitch it into place. Use this hand-stitching to make sure you catch all three layers – the two layers of your cloak and your collar, sandwiched between those two.

48_ Now machine-sew all the way around the neck edge with straight stitch. Your stitches should be catching the outer fabric, the collar, and the lining fabric. Sew slowly, straightening the fabric with your hands as you go so you are not sewing wrinkles into the neck edge.

49_ Trim the corners of your cloak – the two at the neck edge and the two at the bottom of your cloak.

50_ Now put your hand into the gap you left unsewn and drag your whole cloak through that gap, so that the right side emerges into daylight.

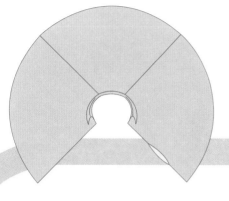

51_ Your collar should be joined to your cloak with a nice neat seam.

52_ Lay your full cloak out and iron all the way around the curved bottom edge. This is a fairly long job, but will give your cloak a nice neat edge. Tug at the edge with your fingertips as you work around so that the stitched join is sitting right at the brink of your cloak edge.

53_ At your unsewn gap, tuck the edges of the fabric into the cloak so they are hidden and so they form one continuous neat straight edge. Iron up each straight edge of your cloak. Sew a line of straight stitch up each straight front edge of your cloak, 2 or 3mm (⅛in) from the edge, to seal this gap and neaten the cloak.

You can insert a zip as described in the hoody instructions (see pages 166–167), add buttons (see page 13), or add a duffle-style fastening (see www.diy-couture. co.uk) to finish your cloak. If you make a long cloak such as the Monochrome Art one (below), create a practical 'sleeve' at each side with a couple of stitches.

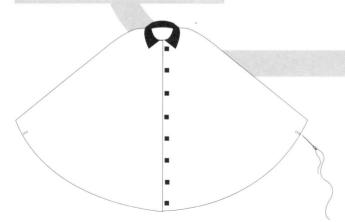

*you have made
a cloak*

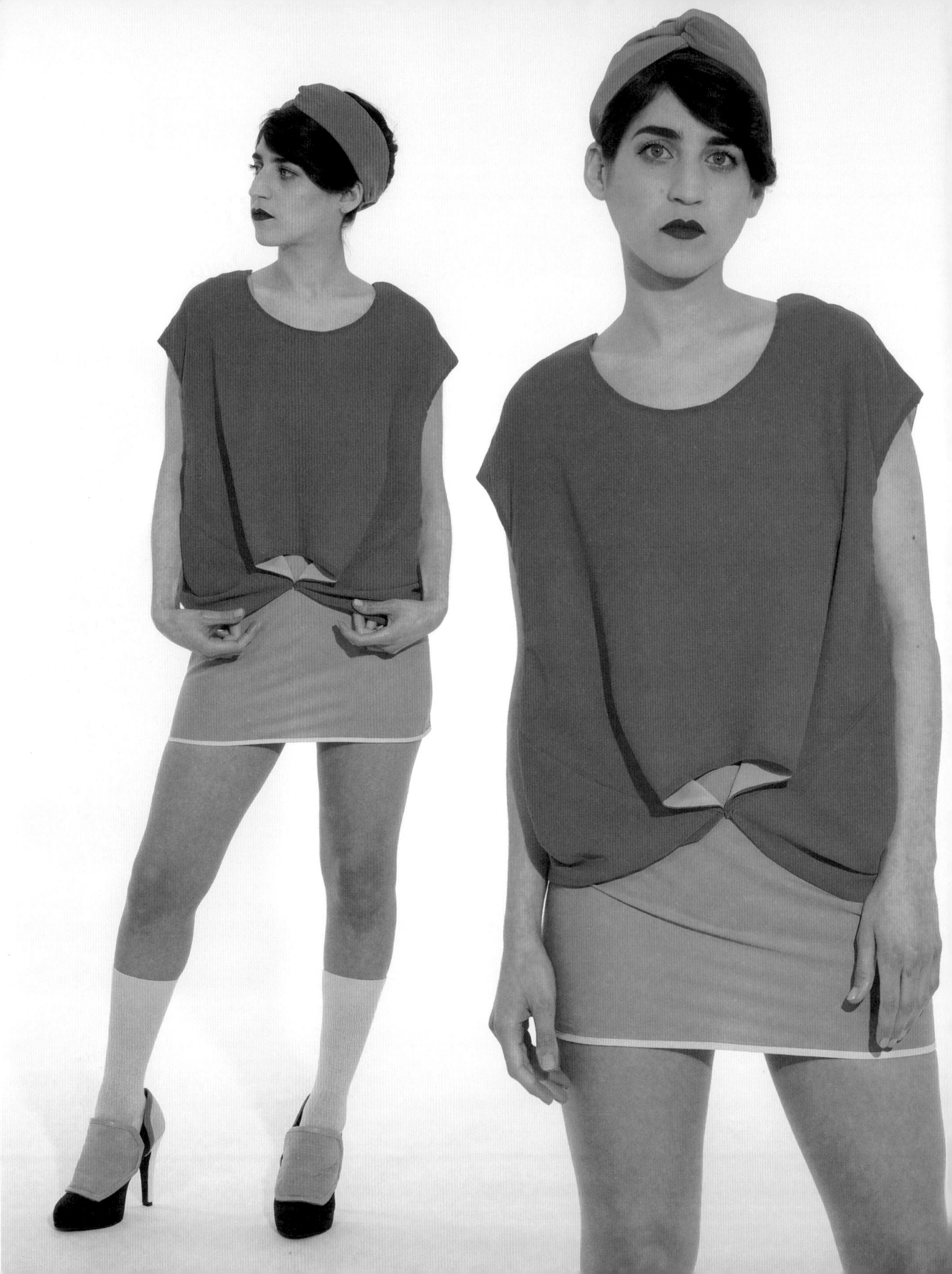

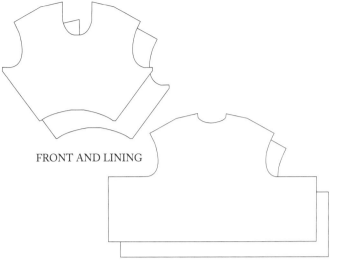

FRONT AND LINING

BACK AND LINING

06.
the slouch top

The slouch top is a baggy, lined top. It is made with a front and back piece and identical pieces cut from lining fabric. The back piece has extended sides that are drawn to the front, hanging in folds. It can be cropped under the bust or made to hang as long as a dress.

TECHNICAL VARIATIONS

the slouch top can be made and worn in a variety of ways

1_ ACID CANDY

2_ MONOCHROME ART

3_ AMERICAN ROAD TRIP

4_ RUDE DISCO

5_ COFFEE CLASSIC

6_ JUNGLE PUNK

7_ SAFARI PREP

8_ TEA PICNIC

1_ ACID CANDY

The Acid Candy slouch top is made of two kinds of chiffon that are both very floppy. The top drapes over the shoulders and covers them. Each shoulder seam measures 19cm (7½in) across. The bottom is shaped into a gentle curve and the two side seams are drawn together to create a sculpted shape that shows a bright dash of the lining fabric. The front piece measures 56cm (22in) before the curve is cut.

2_ MONOCHROME ART

The front of the Monochrome Art slouch top is made using a fairly thick white synthetic fabric on both the outside and inside. The back is entirely made of floppy black suiting fabric. The shoulders are significantly narrower than the Acid Candy slouch top, each one measuring 8cm (3¼in) across. The top is quite long, measuring 63cm (24¾in) from shoulder to bottom, before the curve is cut. The curve is given corners, so that it forms a more graphic, angular outline. The neck is cut in a square shape at the front.

3_ AMERICAN ROAD TRIP

The American Road Trip slouch top is made using a printed cotton on the outside and a plain brushed cotton for the lining. The front piece measures 81cm (32in) deep from shoulder to bottom, before the front curve is cut, so the top falls to the knees almost like a dress. The two side hems are drawn together and hand-stitched to show a splash of the lining fabric.

4_ RUDE DISCO

The Rude Disco slouch top is made of thin, almost transparent, blackish-gold fabric. Despite the jazzy fabric, it has a fairly conservative feel due to an average length (the front pieces measure 53cm/21in from top to bottom), an average shoulder width (it has narrower shoulders than the Acid Candy slouch top, each one measuring 12cm/4¾in across) and a squared bottom – the front is not shaped with a curve.

5_ COFFEE CLASSIC

The Coffee Classic slouch top is made using a heavy jersey-type fabric that has a wrinkle effect. It is lined with a weighty black synthetic fabric that also hangs heavily. The top is cut with narrower shoulders than the Acid Candy top. Each shoulder measures 12.5cm (5in) across. The top itself is fairly short, the front piece measuring 44cm (17¼in) before the curve is cut.

6_ JUNGLE PUNK

The Jungle Punk slouch top is made from a thin but weighty and extremely floppy green fabric. It is lined with a floppy black suiting fabric. The front piece measures 71cm (28in) from shoulder to bottom before the curve is cut. The top has a very deep neckline and narrow shoulders so that it almost appears to be a vest. It has enormous pockets added at the front, each one measuring 28cm (11in) from top to bottom.

7_ SAFARI PREP

The Safari Prep slouch top is made from a medium-weight tweed and lined with a thin shiny red fabric, almost like the fabric hot-air balloons are made from. The top is made with a V-neck. The front piece measures 52cm (20½in) from top to bottom. It is drawn together at the front at a spot that sits inside the side seams.

8_ TEA PICNIC

The Tea Picnic slouch top is made with a light embroidered chiffon and lined with an extremely thin, airy chiffon. It is made to the same dimensions as the Acid Candy slouch top, but the front is not drawn together.

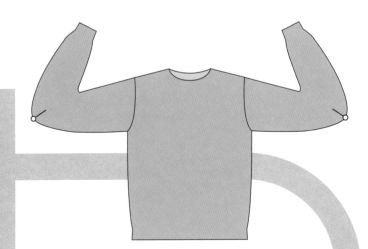

First you are going to mark and cut the front piece.

Find a jumper or long-sleeved T-shirt that fits you snugly at the shoulders and put it on. Take your tape measure and measure the distance from the top shoulder seam of your jumper, at the collar, downwards to your hips. Write this number down. We'll call it your **depth measurement.**

1_ With your jumper still on, bend one of your arms up as if you are showing someone your well-formed bicep. Take a pin with your free hand and put it into your jumper at the bony point of your elbow. Be careful! Do the same on the other side, then take your jumper off.

2_ Now turn to your jumper and fold the arms inwards towards the centre, so the crease lies where you placed your pins.

3_ Lay out your fabric and measure your depth measurement up the vertical edge. Put a pin in there.

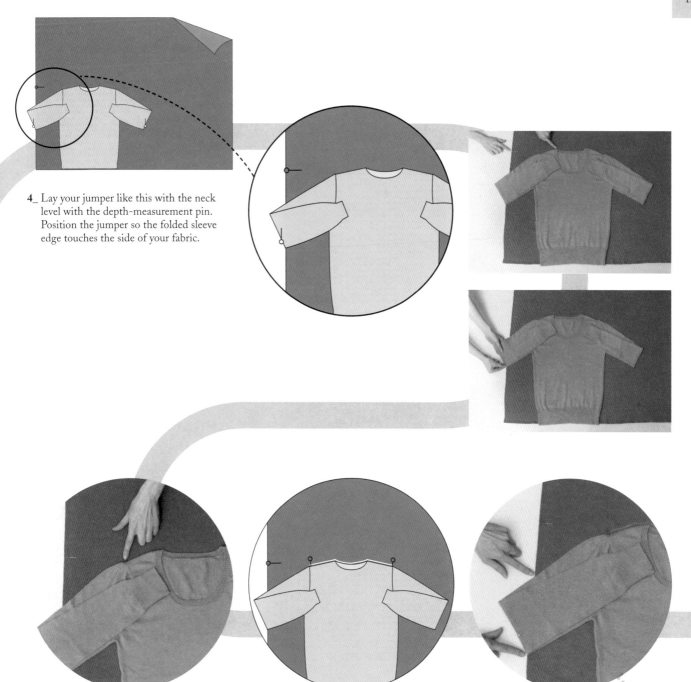

4_ Lay your jumper like this with the neck level with the depth-measurement pin. Position the jumper so the folded sleeve edge touches the side of your fabric.

5_ Put a pin in your fabric at the shoulder point on both sides of your jumper.

6_ Draw around the jumper with your tailor's chalk from shoulder pin to shoulder pin.

7_ Put a pin into your fabric where the top and bottom of the folded sleeve meet the edge of your fabric.

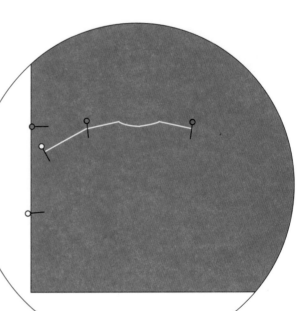

8_ Measure 5cm (2in) along the top of the sleeve, from the edge of your fabric inwards, and put a pin in there.

9_ Draw a line from this pin to your shoulder pin, following the slope of your sleeve and joining the chalk line you have already made. You can now put your jumper to one side.

You need to finish marking the rest of your shape. First, you need to mark your armhole.

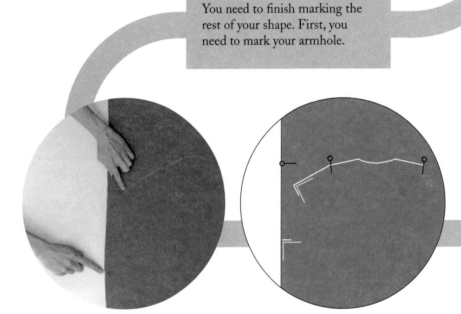

10_ Draw short straight lines of about 4cm (1½in) at your arm pins. The lines should form right-angle corners with the side of your fabric and the shoulder line. The right angles are marked in yellow on the diagram.

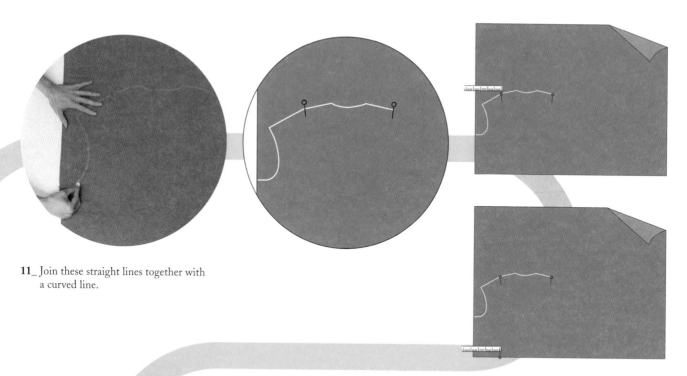

11_ Join these straight lines together with a curved line.

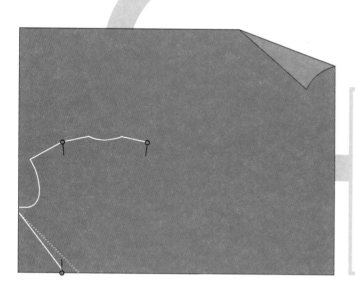

12_ Now measure the distance your left shoulder pin sits inland from the edge of your fabric and put a pin in the bottom edge of your fabric at the same distance from the edge (directly below your shoulder pin).

You can create a steeper diagonal line here, which stretches further inland, beyond the point parallel with your shoulder pin. This will make your top narrower at the front, like the Monochrome Art and Jungle Punk slouch tops. A very narrow front piece will not allow you to pinch the top together at the very end of the slouch top making process. Have a look at the variations on pages 110–111 to help you decide how you want to mark your shape.

13_ Draw a line sloping diagonally upwards from this pin to the lower sleeve pin at the edge of your fabric. You can use your tape measure or a sheet of paper or newspaper to help you draw a straight line.

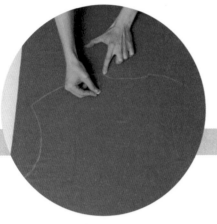

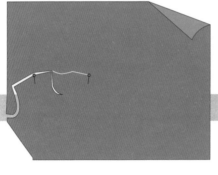

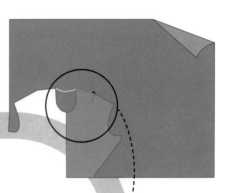

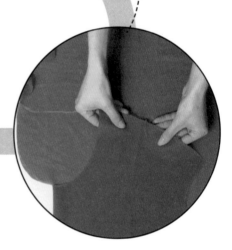

14_ Deepen the neckline by drawing a curve to the centre of your piece – a process explained in greater details in the Grecian dress instructions on pages 54–55.

15_ Cut around the half you have now drawn and fold it over to the right, matching up your shoulder points and the horizontal bottom edge of your fabric.

16_ Use the folded side of your shape to cut the second side exactly the same.

You can choose to cut a deep or a shallow curve – or no curve at all – to change the shape of your slouch top at the front. Look at the variations on pages 110–111 to help you decide how big you want your curve. The curve shown here is 6cm (2½in) deep.

17_ If you want to cut a curved shape at the bottom of your front piece, mark the depth of the curve you want up the vertical folded edge of the piece. The wrong side of the material should be facing you.

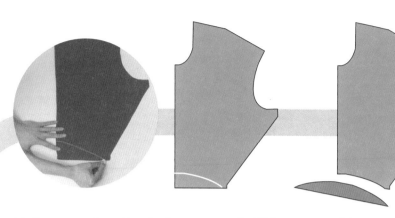

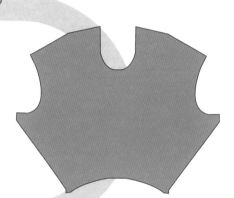

18_ Draw a curve from this point down towards the bottom corner of your piece.

19_ With your piece still folded, cut along the line you have marked. You will be cutting through two layers of fabric.

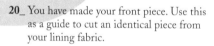

Now use the front piece as a guide to cutting your back piece.

20_ You have made your front piece. Use this as a guide to cut an identical piece from your lining fabric.

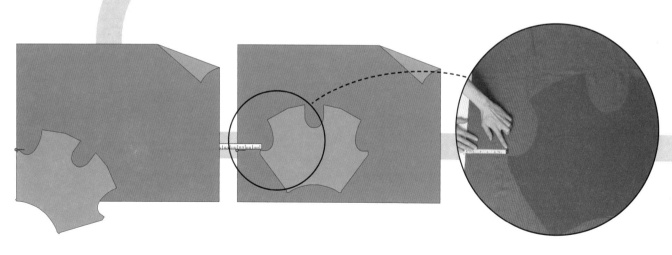

21_ Take your front piece and lay it so the sloping side edge runs parallel with the side of your uncut fabric. Put a pin in your fabric to mark this distance.

22_ Now shift your front piece so that it sits straight (rather than at a diagonal angle). Push it inland an extra 15cm (6in) and put a couple of pins in so that it sits still.

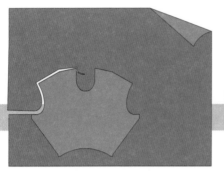

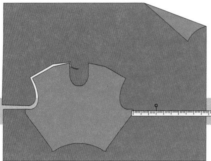

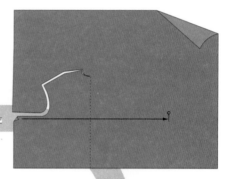

23_ Cut a straight line in from the edge of your fabric to your armpit point then around your armhole, your sloping shoulder edge, and half of your neck edge. Make the neck edge fairly shallow (shallower than your front piece), to stop the top slipping off your shoulders.

24_ Measure 15cm (6in) horizontally outwards from the right armpit point and put a pin in to mark the spot.

25_ Remove your front piece and put it to one side. You are going to flip the half of the piece you have just cut over to the right.

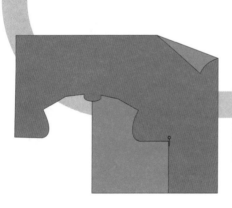

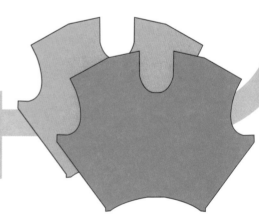

Now you are going to join each outer piece to its corresponding lining piece.

26_ Line up the armpit corner with the pin you have just put in, then use this folded half as a guide to cutting the second half of your back piece. Use this as a guide to cut an identical piece from your lining fabric.

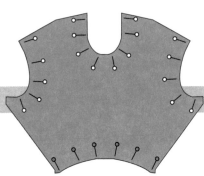

27_ Lay your front lining piece out with the right side of the fabric facing upwards and lay your outer front piece on top of it with the right side facing down. You should be looking at the wrong side of your fabric.

28_ Pin the two pieces together along the curved arm edges, the curved neck edge, and along the curved bottom edge.

29_ Sew your two front pieces together along these pinned edges.

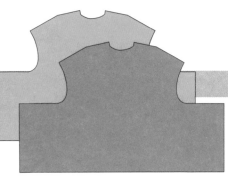

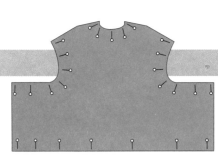

30_ You have made a sort of front piece pocket.

31_ Repeat this process with your back pieces, pinning the outer to the lining at the curved arm edges, the curved neck edge, and the long straight bottom edge.

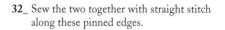

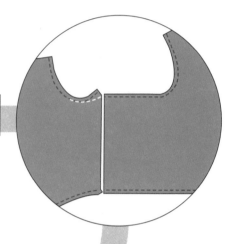

32_ Sew the two together with straight stitch along these pinned edges.

33_ Take your front piece and compare the length of the sloping line at the side to the corresponding straight line at the side of your back piece.

34_ You are going to join these together and they need to be the same length. Check both sides for length variations. If one piece is longer, you can sew a line of stitching further inland so that it becomes shorter.

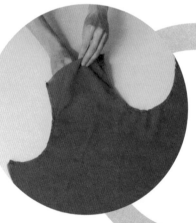

35_ With your side lengths even, put your hand into your front piece and pull it the right way round, so that all the edges you have just sewn disappear to the inside.

36_ Lay your piece out and iron all the joined edges so that they are neat and flat.

37_ It is easier to be neat if you iron your seams while looking at the lining fabric, so that you can see your lining is sitting on top of or just inside your outer fabric.

Your shoulder edges and sides will still be raw and unjoined. You are now going to join the front piece to the back piece along these edges.

38_ Repeat this with your back piece so that you have a neatly lined front and back.

39_ Lay your back piece out with your outer fabric facing upwards towards you. Lay your front piece on top of it with the outer fabric facing down. You should be looking at the lining fabric of your front piece.

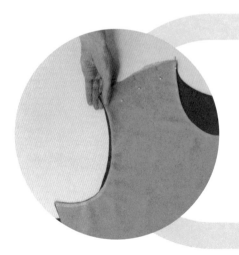

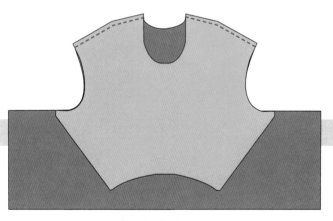

40_ Pin your front piece to your back piece along the sloping shoulder edges, aligning the raw edges as accurately as you can. As in step 34, if your shoulder widths are wildly different at the front and back, you can turn the offending larger piece inside out and sew lines of straight stitch to make the area narrower.

41_ Sew the front and back pieces together with a line of straight stitch running about 1.5cm (⅝in) away from the edge.

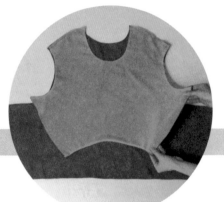

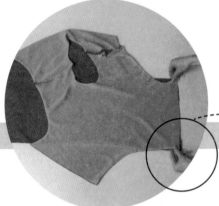

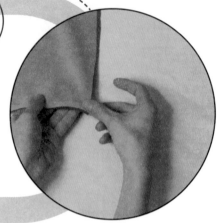

42_ Lay your piece out again and drag one sloping side of your front piece down and sideways until it matches up with the corresponding vertical side edge of your back piece.

43_ Line up the two bottom edges as accurately as you can for a neat appearance.

44_ Pin the two together, then sew them together with straight stitch.

You can wear your slouch top like this, or you can draw the side seams together at the front and join them with a couple of hand-stitches. This will bring the top in at the back and create an elegant folded curve at the front that displays your lining fabric.

45_ Repeat this process with the other unsewn side. Zigzag both side seams together, push to one side and sew flat with a line of straight stitch, as detailed in the Grecian dress instructions on page 56.

46_ Lay your slouch top out so you are looking at the front and take hold of the side seams.

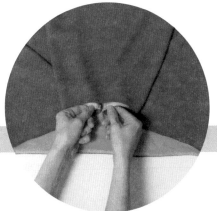

47_ Bring your hands towards the centre of the garment, bringing the two seams together.

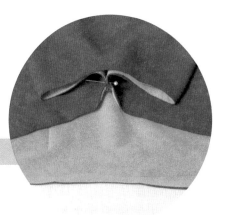

48_ Pin the two sides of the garment together with just one pin, slightly above the two seams.

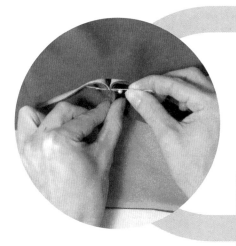

49_ Put a couple of hand-stitches in here to hold the fold in place.

You can also add pockets to your slouch top. See pages 16–17 for guidance on making and positioning pockets.

you have made a slouch top

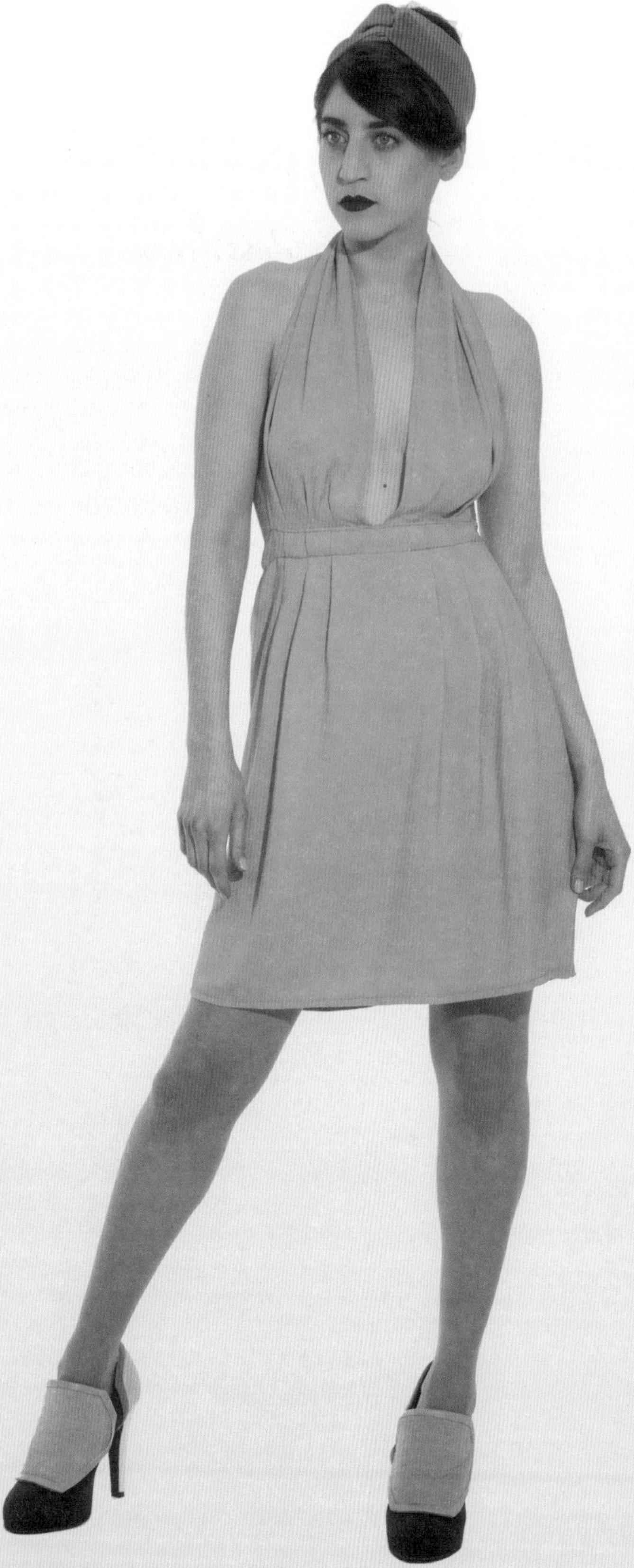

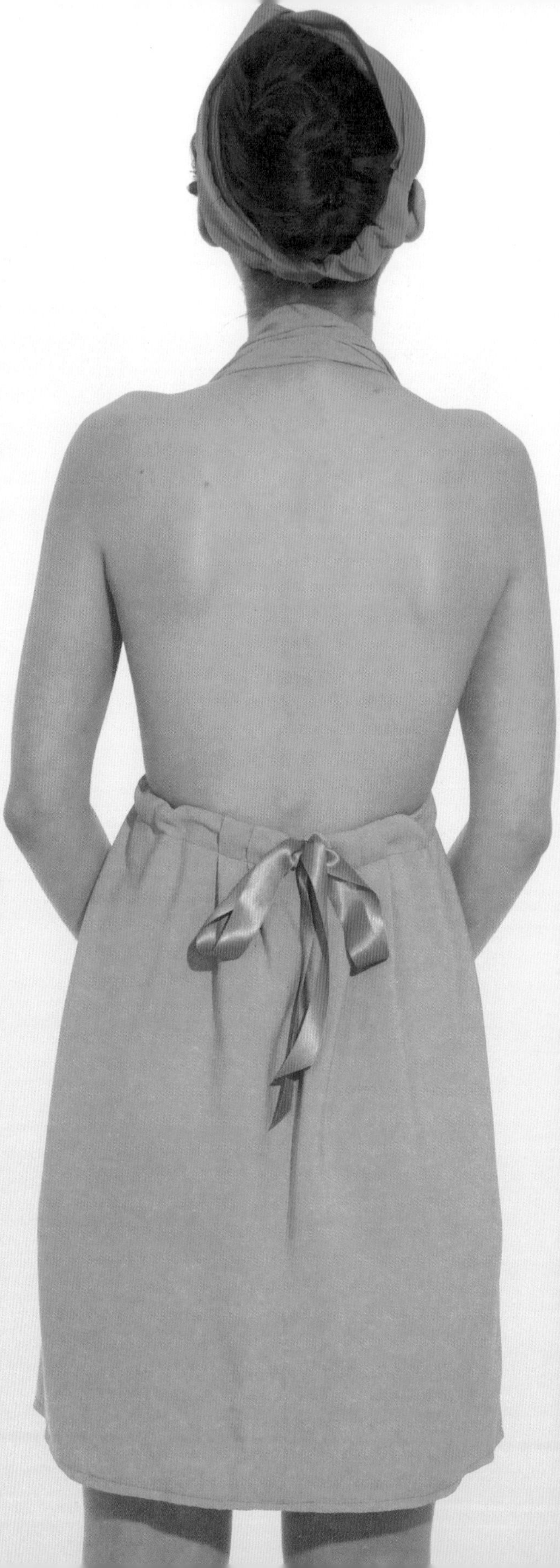

SKIRT PIECE

BUST PIECE

07.

the goddess dress

The goddess dress is an elegant piece simply made of two rectangles of fabric: a long bust piece that forms a halterneck, and a pleated skirt piece that wraps all the way around your body. It can fasten with a ribbon – either threaded through the dress or attached to the dress – which ties at the back, or be secured with elastic.

TECHNICAL VARIATIONS

the goddess dress can be made and worn in a variety of ways

1_ ACID CANDY

2_ MONOCHROME ART

3_ AMERICAN ROAD TRIP

4_ RUDE DISCO

5_ COFFEE CLASSIC

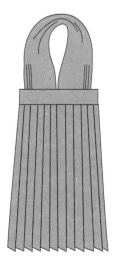

6_ JUNGLE PUNK

7_ SAFARI PREP

8_ TEA PICNIC

1_ ACID CANDY

The Acid Candy goddess dress is made from a floppy synthetic fabric. The skirt piece is cut 60cm (23½in) deep. The top of the skirt piece has a 3.5cm (1⅜in)-deep hem through which a piece of ribbon is threaded. This ties the dress at the back. The skirt piece has six pleats across the front (three on each side), each using about 6cm (2½in) of fabric. There are four pleats at the back. The bust piece is fairly narrow; it is made from a strip of fabric 24cm (9½in) wide. It has three tucks on either side, each using about 3cm (1¼in) of fabric. The two ends do not meet, revealing the chest down to the waist.

2_ MONOCHROME ART

The Monochrome Art goddess dress is made using two contrasting fabrics. The skirt part of the dress is made of light synthetic black fabric that drifts in folds. It has been hand-screenprinted. It has four deep pleats across the front, each one using 8cm (3¼in) of fabric. The bust piece is cut 24cm (9½in) wide – the same as the Acid Candy bust piece – but it has been sewn so there is almost no gap between the pieces in the centre. The dress has a short piece of ribbon sewn to each side of the opening at the back, which fastens in a bow.

3_ AMERICAN ROAD TRIP

The American Road Trip goddess dress is made from a fairly thin but tough fabric with an Aztec-style print. The skirt piece is cut 110cm (43in) deep so that it almost sweeps the floor. It has eight pleats at the front, each using about 4cm (1½in) of fabric. The bust piece is also cut long, at 110cm (43in), so that it comes right down to the waist. It has four evenly spaced tucks on each side. The bust piece is sewn so that the two central edges slightly overlap, completely covering the chest.

4_ RUDE DISCO

The skirt part of the Rude Disco goddess dress is made of thick magenta fabric woven from metallic threads. It has been cut short to give it a flamboyant party feel. It has three pleats on each side, one using 5cm (2in) of fabric and two using 8cm (3¼in). The bust part is made of fairly thick navy satin and has three 1cm (⅜in) pleats on each side. The bust piece is cut 28cm (11in) wide and is sewn with a 4cm (1½in) gap in the middle. The tie is thick black satin. It is 7cm (2¾in) deep and a popper or press-stud is used to fasten it at the back.

5_ COFFEE CLASSIC

The Coffee Classic goddess dress is made using a thin, stiff fabric. The skirt hangs slightly above the knees. The strip of fabric used for the skirt piece is very wide at 152cm (60in). It has 18 pleats, each using about 6cm (2½in) of fabric, which are ironed in one by one. This is time-consuming, but creates a dramatic effect. The bust piece is narrow at 21.5cm (8½in) wide. It has three tiny pleats on each side, at the outer edge of the body. The finished waistband is deep at 8cm (3¼in).

6_ JUNGLE PUNK

The Jungle Punk goddess dress is made from three fabrics. The skirt is light poplin polycotton, and is short with a large 5cm (2in) hem at the top, through which thick elastic is threaded. It has four large pleats at the front, each using about 10cm (4in) of fabric. The bust piece is made from two contrasting fabrics that are joined to form one long strip (see page 136). The bust piece overlaps slightly in the centre. It has two pleats on each side, each pleat using about 3cm (1¼in) of fabric.

7_ SAFARI PREP

The Safari Prep goddess dress is made from a tan fabric with a vintage feel. The skirt piece is fairly short. It is not hemmed at bottom or top; the edges are finished with bias binding. The bias binding at the top of the skirt piece is added before the bust piece is attached, and makes a tie at the back of the dress. The bust piece, also finished with bias binding, is a wide 30cm (12in) across, and is long, at 98cm (38½in), so the skirt sits at the waist. The bust pieces overlap slightly at the centre. Contrasting maroon pockets give the dress a practical look.

8_ TEA PICNIC

The knee-length Tea Picnic goddess dress is made from slightly transparent fabric, so the bust piece is cut to double the intended width, folded with the right side of the fabric on the inside, and the long edges pinned and sewn together, creating a double-thickness tube. It is 24cm (9½in) wide when finished and overlaps at the centre, covering the chest area. The skirt piece has several small pleats of random size, made before the piece is cut. The tie for this dress is a waistband, as described in the straight skirt instructions (see page 43), just 2.5cm (1in) deep. It is 40cm (15¾in) longer than the waist and ties in a bow at the back.

First you are going to mark and cut the skirt piece of your dress. The skirt piece is a rectangle that wraps around your body, joining at the back. Start by measuring the full distance around your body under your breasts, or wherever you would like your dress to sit. The dress sits very comfortably on an 'inny' bit of your body, or on a ledge. If you want it to sit under your bust, it will need to be tied tightly, or you can use elastic rather than a ribbon to keep it up. In the dress photographed, this measurement is 76cm (30in). Write this number down. We'll call it your **full-body measurement**.

The skirt piece has pleats to add shape and give you room to move. If you have wide hips, make sure you add enough pleats to accommodate them. Decide how many pleats you would like to put into your dress. The dress pictured has six pleats at the front (three on each side) and four at the back (two on each side). Each pleat takes up 5cm (2in) of fabric. (You can make your pleats bigger or smaller than this – the variations on the previous page may help you decide.) So ten pleats, each taking up 5cm (2in) of fabric, means that an additional 50cm (20in) of fabric was added to the full-body measurement. Look over the page to help you visualize where the pleats will sit.

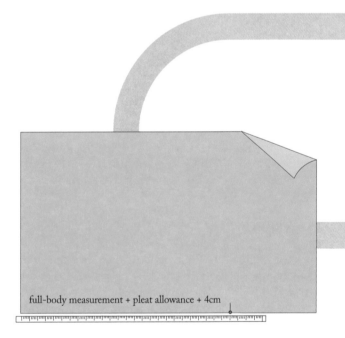

full-body measurement + pleat allowance + 4cm

1_ Measure your full body measurement plus your pleat allowance (126cm/50in in this case), plus an extra 4cm (1½in) for seams across your fabric and put a pin in there.

Now hold the end of your tape measure under your bust, or wherever the skirt part of your dress is going to sit, and let it hang down. Decide how long you would like your dress to be and look at the measurement there. Write this down. You also need to decide at this point whether you are threading a ribbon through your dress. If you are, you will add a hem at the top of your skirt piece that is deep enough to push the ribbon through. You need to add enough fabric for this to the length of your skirt piece. See the following box for guidance.

The dress pictured has an orange ribbon 2.5cm (1in) deep. 4cm (1½in) was added to the initial length measurement to allow for this. This meant 4cm (1½in) of fabric could be folded over and a line of stitching made sitting 1cm (⅜in) inside this fold, leaving room to push the ribbon through.

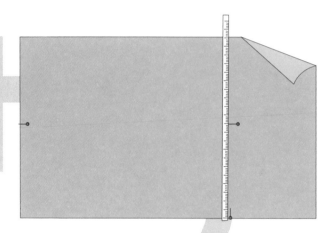

2_ Measure your length measurement plus any hem allowance up the side of your fabric and upwards from the first pin you positioned. Put pins in both places.

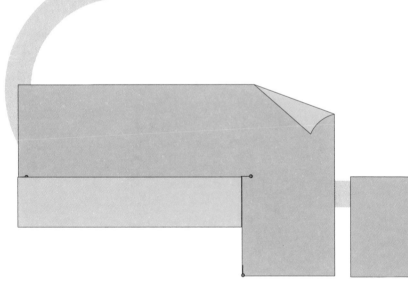

3_ Cut upwards into your fabric from the first pin, then fold this long rectangular flap of fabric upwards to help you cut a straight line across the top of your dress piece.

4_ You now have a large rectangle, which will become the skirt part of your dress.

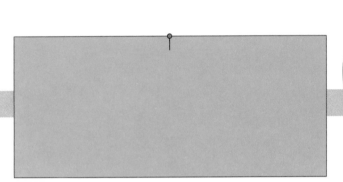
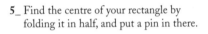

5_ Find the centre of your rectangle by folding it in half, and put a pin in there.

6_ You will make your front pleats on either side of this pin. Nip a bit of fabric between your fingers on one side of the pin and continue nipping it so you form an even ridge running about 15cm (6in) down your rectangle.

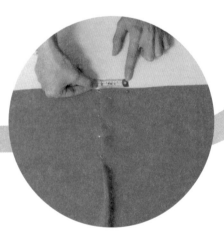

7_ Check with your fingers that the pleat itself is squared and that both sides are running parallel, then add a few more pins to keep the fold in place.

8_ Use your tape measure to check that your pleat uses the amount of fabric that you planned to use. Remember, you don't have to aim for perfection – just check that the pleats are roughly the right size.

9_ Measure how far away the peak of your pleat is from the central pin, then make a mark the same distance away on the other side.

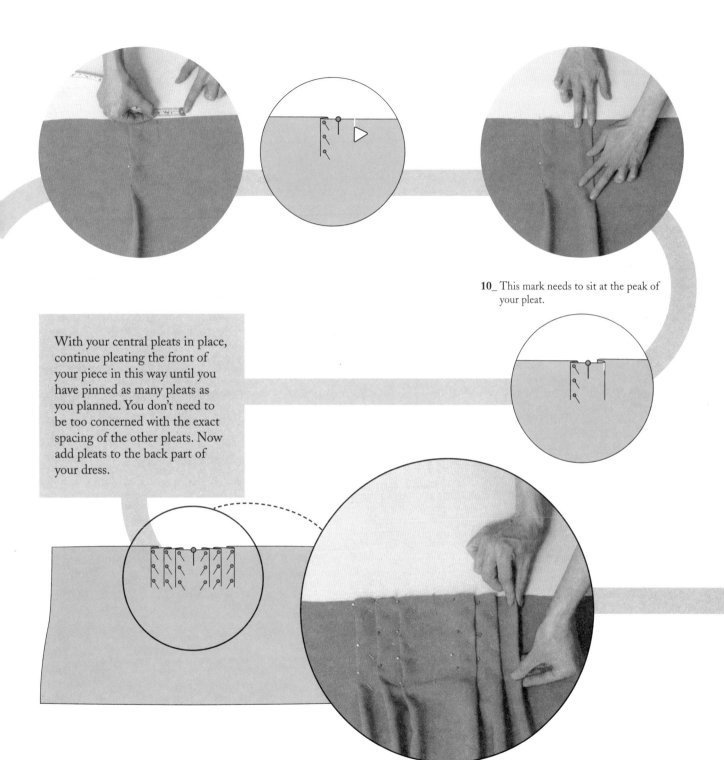

10_ This mark needs to sit at the peak of your pleat.

With your central pleats in place, continue pleating the front of your piece in this way until you have pinned as many pleats as you planned. You don't need to be too concerned with the exact spacing of the other pleats. Now add pleats to the back part of your dress.

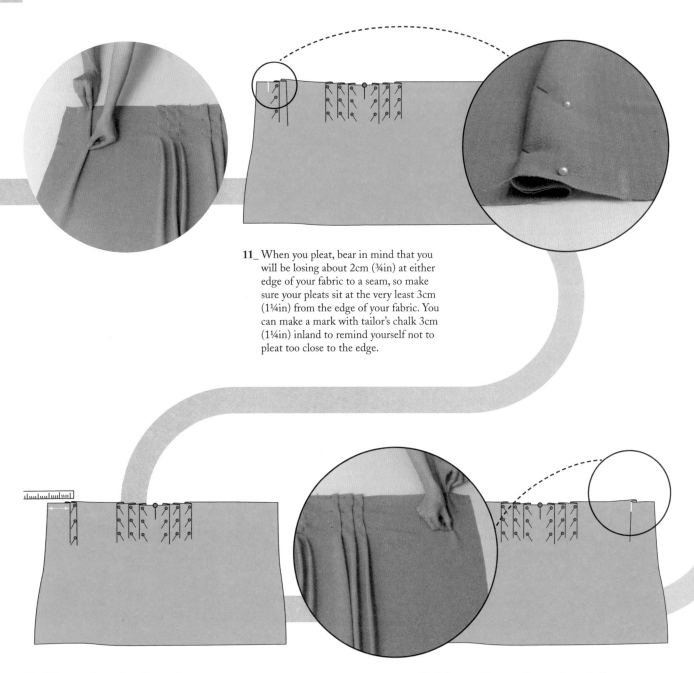

11_ When you pleat, bear in mind that you will be losing about 2cm (¾in) at either edge of your fabric to a seam, so make sure your pleats sit at the very least 3cm (1¼in) from the edge of your fabric. You can make a mark with tailor's chalk 3cm (1¼in) inland to remind yourself not to pleat too close to the edge.

12_ When you have pinned your pleats on one side, measure how far inland the peak of your first pleat sits from the edge of your fabric.

13_ Measure this same distance inwards from the other side of your skirt piece and make a mark with tailor's chalk. This is going to be the peak of your pleat. Pinch it between your fingers and drag it over to form a pleat. Pin it down and check that it uses roughly the same amount of fabric as the first pleat on the other side of your skirt piece.

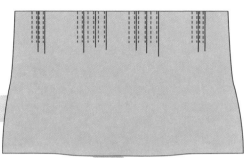

15_ With your pleats pinned in, sew down both sides of your pleat – the folded edge you can see and the folded edge you can't – with a long straight stitch. Sew downwards double the length of the hem you are going to make at the top, plus about an extra 1cm (⅜in). If you are adding a fabric belt instead, sew downwards about 3cm (1¼in). There is no need to finish these lines by running your stitches backwards, as you will unpick them later. Zigzag-stitch all the way along your long pleated edge.

14_ Once you have pinned the pleats on both outer sides of your skirt piece, use your hand or your eyes – or if you really want to be accurate, a tape measure – to check that the pleats sit about the same distance away from your front pleats on both sides of the piece.

Next, you need to turn your rectangle into a tube by joining the two vertical edges together.

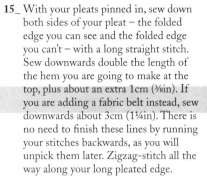

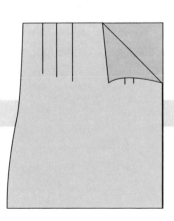

16_ Fold your pleated rectangle in half with the right side of the fabric hidden on the inside. Line up the two vertical edges.

17_ You need to leave about 20cm (8in) at the top unjoined, to allow yourself an opening to climb into the dress. Measure this distance plus the amount you need to leave for a hem (for a ribbon tie) down your skirt piece from the top.

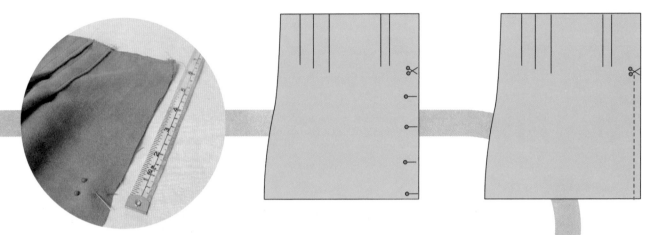

18_ Put a couple of pins in here, to remind yourself to stop sewing when you reach this point.

19_ Now pin the edges together all the way down to the bottom.

20_ Sew the two edges together with a line of straight stitch running about 2cm (¾in) in from the edge. (This is slightly wider than a normal hem.)

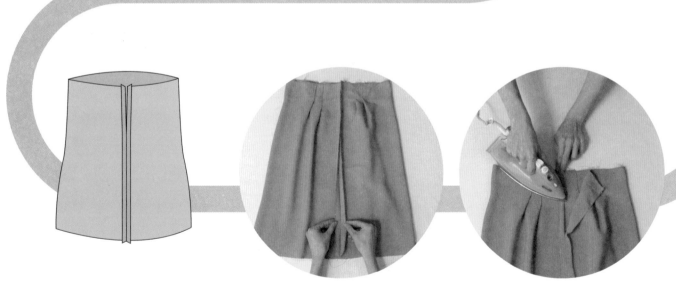

21_ Open the flaps of the seam you have just made and iron them so that they sit flat.

22_ Continue ironing the flaps of fabric, beyond the part you have sewn, to create two straight pressed edges.

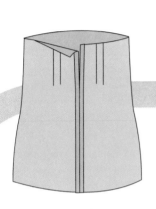

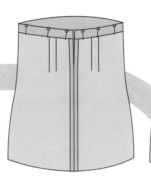

23_ If you are going to thread a ribbon through your dress you can now hem your pleated edge. Make sure you fold a hem that is wide enough for your ribbon, and pin in place.

24_ Sew the fold down with straight stitch close to the zigzagged edge.

25_ If you are adding a fabric belt to your dress, make a waistband in the way described in the straight skirt instructions on pages 43–45. Make sure the strip of fabric you cut is about 50cm (20in) longer than the distance around the pleated edge of your skirt piece. This will allow you about 20cm (8in) on each side to tie into a knot or bow. Attach the waistband in the way described in the straight skirt instructions, sandwiching the pleated edge of your skirt piece between the front and back of your folded belt. Remember to leave that extra overhang at each side.

Now it is time to make the bust part of your dress. Take your tape measure and droop it over your neck so that the end hangs where the top of the main body of your dress will sit. Hold your tape measure so that it doesn't bypass the curve of your breasts (i.e. so it is not hanging directly over the flatter, central part of your chest, but follows the swell of your chest). Look at the measurement and add an extra 10cm (4in) to this. Mark this distance along your fabric. The dress here uses an initial bust measurement of 82cm (32¼in), then adds an extra 10cm (4in) to make 92cm (36¼in). This is the length of the long rectangle that makes up the bust piece.

The bust piece can be wider or narrower, to create different looks. See the variations on pages 126–127 to help you decide. The Jungle Punk bust piece is made of two strips of different coloured fabric joined so the seam sits at the back of the neck. Decide how long your bust piece will be, then cut two pieces, each half this length. Join them as described in the bias binding section on page 14, to give you one long strip, and continue from step 27.

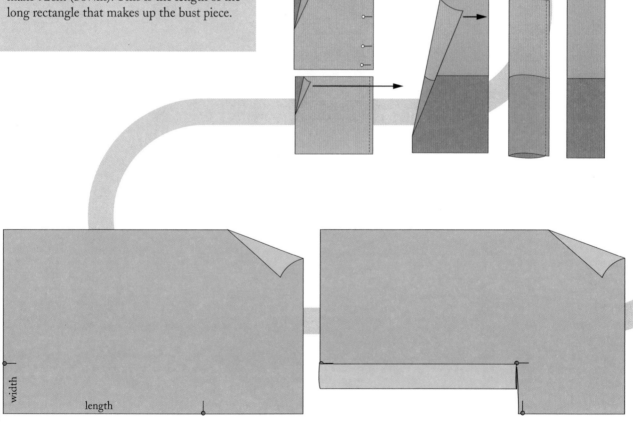

26_ The bust rectangle needs to be as wide as a quarter of your initial full-body measurement, plus an additional 5cm (2in) to allow for hemming. Measure this distance up your fabric and cut your rectangle, folding up the long straight edge of the fabric and using it as a guide to cut the second long edge.

You are going to hem each of the long straight edges of your bust piece. As an alternative, you can bypass this hemming part and instead finish your edges with a decorative bias binding. This is demonstrated on the Safari Prep goddess dress; see page 126.

27_ You need to make a fairly narrow hem – about 5mm (¼in) – that is folded over on itself (folded twice) to hide the raw edge of your fabric.

28_ Fold about 5mm (¼in) over first and iron this fold into place, all the way up one long edge of the bust piece.

29_ Then take this folded edge and fold it over again, so that you are hiding the raw edge. Iron this second fold into place with a bit of extra muscle, or some steam.

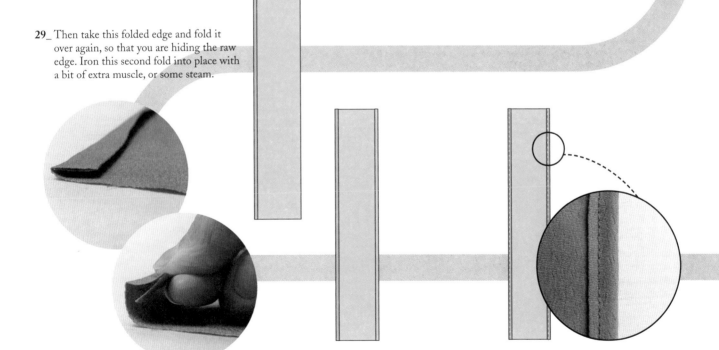

30_ Repeat this hemming process on the other long edge of your rectangle.

31_ Sew your folds down with a line of straight stitch running close to the folded edge of your fabric.

Now you need to make some small tucks at each unhemmed end of your bust piece. These help make a full three-dimensional shape for your breasts. The dress shown here has three tucks at each end, each using 2cm (¾in) of fabric. The tucks are evenly spaced across the bust piece.

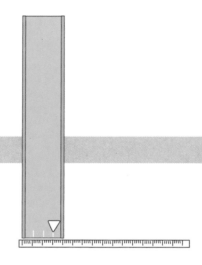

32_ Make marks with tailor's chalk roughly evenly spaced across the end of your bust piece. Start by marking a central line to help you space the other tucks evenly.

33_ Tweak your fabric at one of the lines you have marked and pull it up, folding your fabric along the line you have drawn.

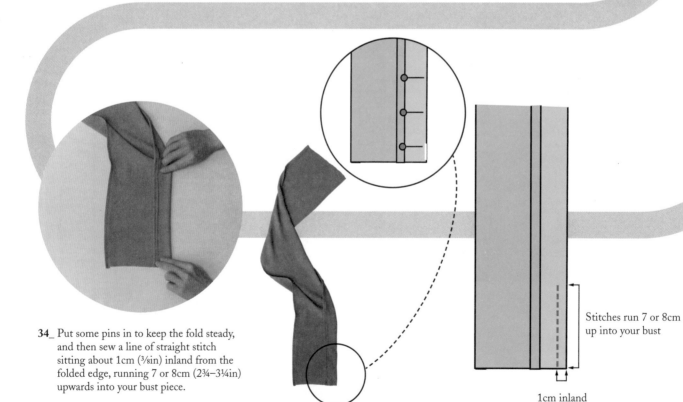

34_ Put some pins in to keep the fold steady, and then sew a line of straight stitch sitting about 1cm (³⁄₈in) inland from the folded edge, running 7 or 8cm (2¾–3¼in) upwards into your bust piece.

Stitches run 7 or 8cm up into your bust

1cm inland

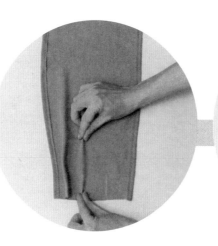

35_ Repeat these steps until you have made
the number of tucks you want.

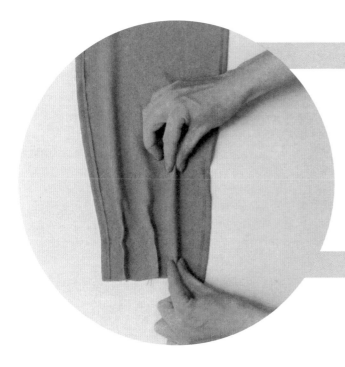

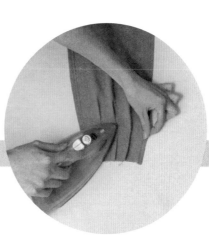

36_ Push your tucks over to one side so that
they sit flat, and press them down with an
iron so that they stay that way.

Now you are going to make tucks in a similar position at the other end of your bust piece. The intention here is to enable you to make evenly spaced tucks. You can make randomly spaced, roughly even tucks if you prefer; the bust piece will still look good.

37_ Lay your bust piece out with the wrong side facing upwards (you should be able to see all the messy bits of your tucks) and fold the tucked end over towards the end you haven't yet touched.

You are going to use the tucks you have made as a guide to position your second set of tucks.

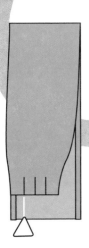

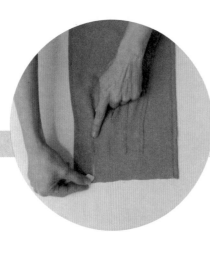

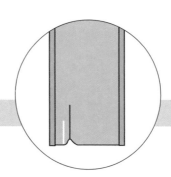

38_ Make a mark with your tailor's chalk where the join of your first tuck sits. This is going to form the bottom – not the peak – of the tuck you are now making.

39_ The fabric you are scooping into the tuck needs to be taken entirely from beyond the mark you have made.

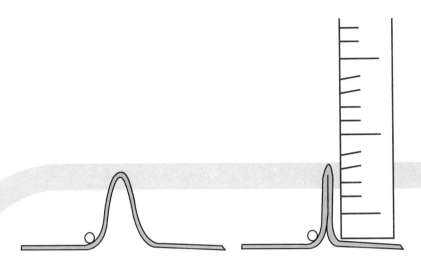

40_ You can see a cross-section of that here; the white ball indicates your line of tailor's chalk.

41_ If you used 2cm (¾in) of fabric to make tucks that were 1cm (⅜in) deep on the other side of your bust piece, you need to do that here too.

42_ Pin and sew this tuck.

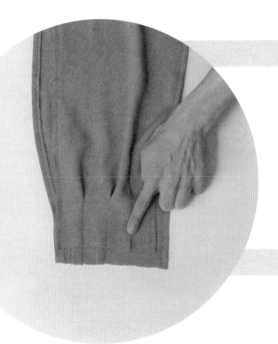

43_ Mark, pin and sew your second and third pleats in the same way as you did the first, with the tailor's chalk mark sitting at the base of your tucks.

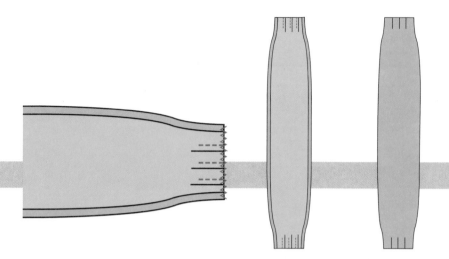

You need to join your bust piece
to the skirt piece of your dress.

44_ Iron your tucks flat and run over each end
with zigzag stitch.

45_ You now have a complete, shaped
bust piece.

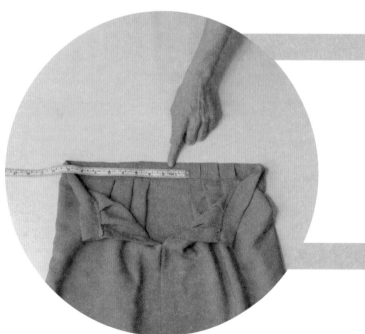

46_ Find the front central point of your dress
and put a pin in there.

47_ Position one end of your bust piece to one
side of your central pin, on the wrong side
of your fabric. You should be looking at
the wrong side of your bust piece.

The bust piece shown here was positioned exactly on the central pin. When it was angled down, the central edges moved away from the centre pin, and the piece was sewn into position with a gap in the centre. You could also overlap the two sides of your bust piece, or leave a large gap between them. See the variations on pages 126–127 to help you decide.

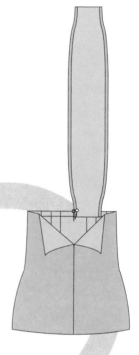

48_ Pin the inner side of your bust piece to your skirt piece.

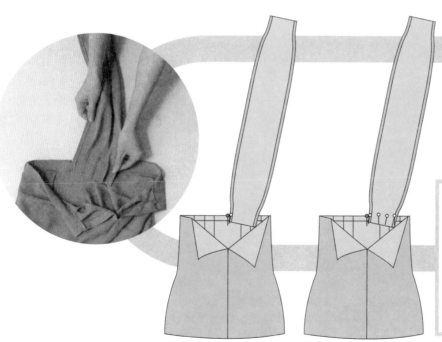

You can choose to attach your bust piece without angling the ends. The bust piece on the Safari Prep dress has not been angled. It clings to the chest more tightly all the way up, rather than hanging slightly open at the centre.

49_ Then pull the outer side downwards slightly – about 3 or 4cm (1¼–1½in).

50_ This means the bottom edges of your bust piece will sit at an angle rather than perfectly horizontal. This will give your bust piece a bit of extra shape, making it hang away slightly from the middle.

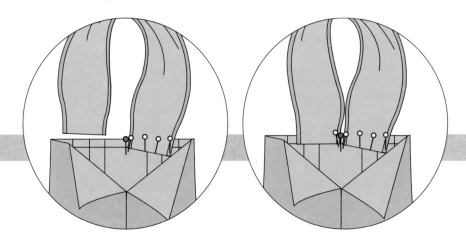

51_ Now spread your dress so you can access the other side easily.

52_ Make sure your bust piece is not twisted, unless you want it to be. Position the second side an equal distance from the middle and pin it into place.

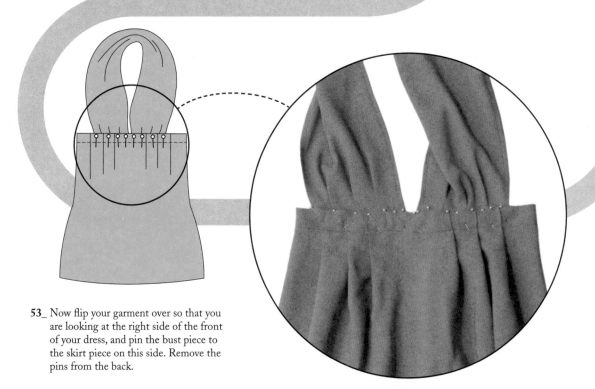

53_ Now flip your garment over so that you are looking at the right side of the front of your dress, and pin the bust piece to the skirt piece on this side. Remove the pins from the back.

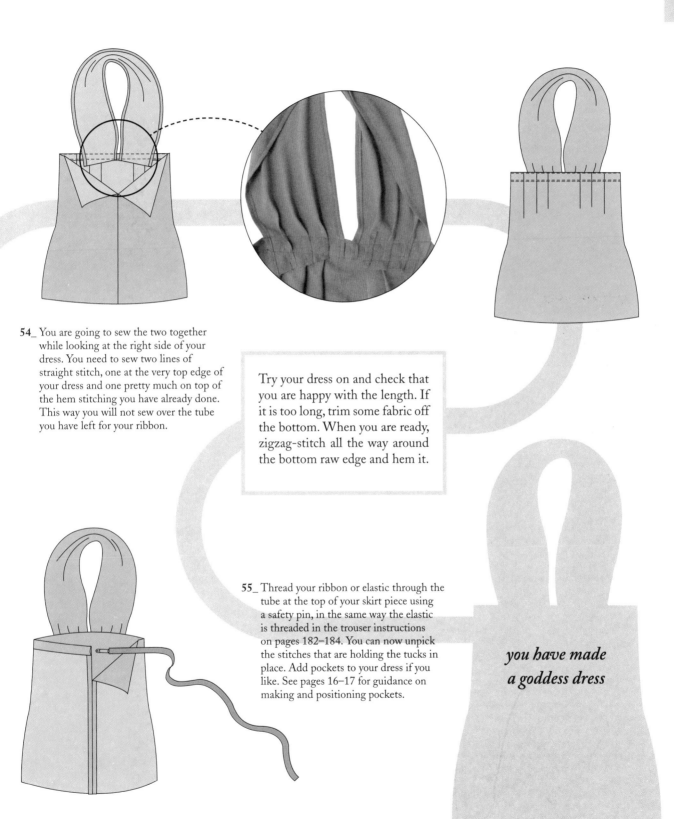

54_ You are going to sew the two together while looking at the right side of your dress. You need to sew two lines of straight stitch, one at the very top edge of your dress and one pretty much on top of the hem stitching you have already done. This way you will not sew over the tube you have left for your ribbon.

Try your dress on and check that you are happy with the length. If it is too long, trim some fabric off the bottom. When you are ready, zigzag-stitch all the way around the bottom raw edge and hem it.

55_ Thread your ribbon or elastic through the tube at the top of your skirt piece using a safety pin, in the same way the elastic is threaded in the trouser instructions on pages 182–184. You can now unpick the stitches that are holding the tucks in place. Add pockets to your dress if you like. See pages 16–17 for guidance on making and positioning pockets.

you have made a goddess dress

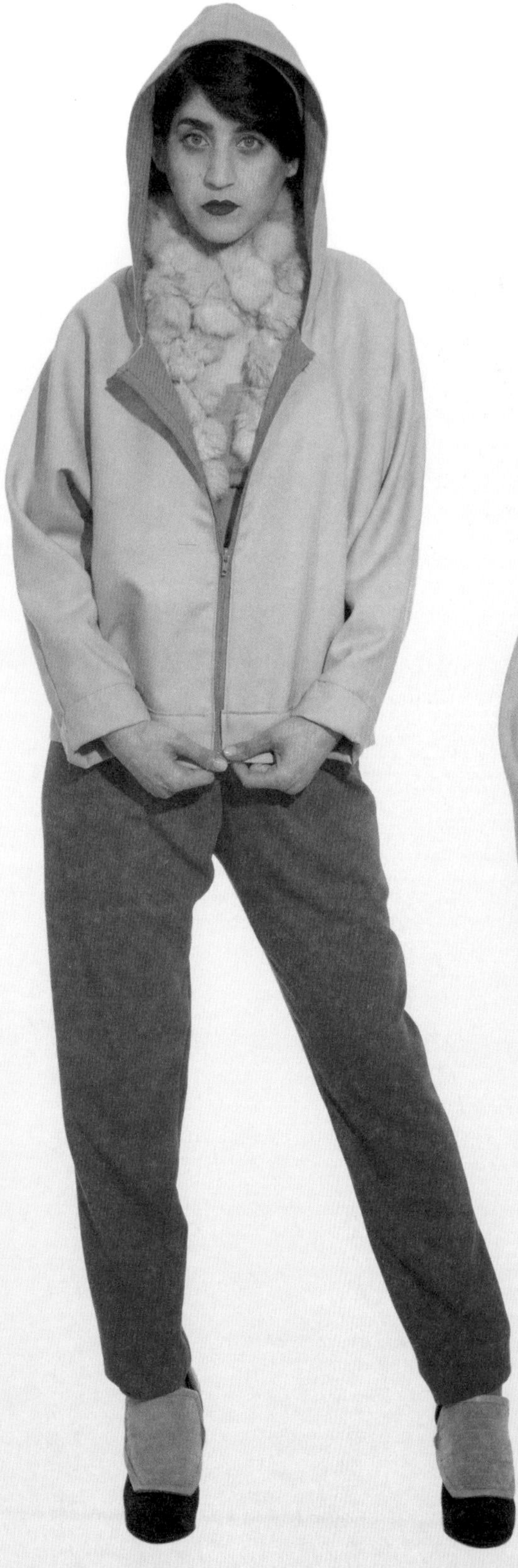

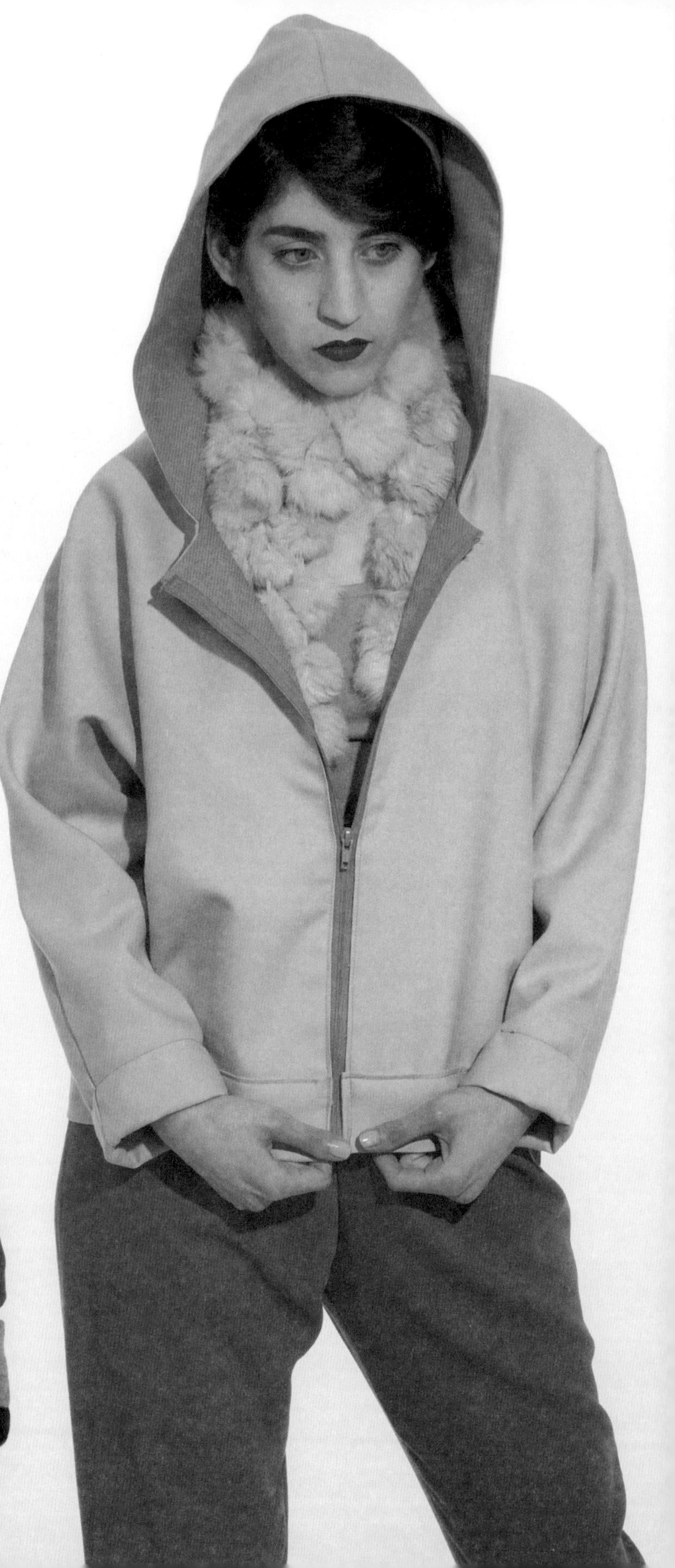

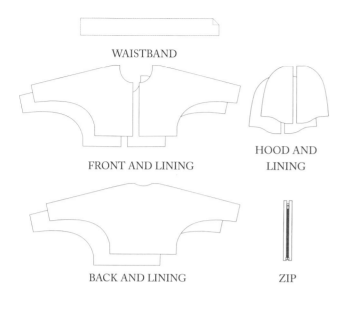

WAISTBAND

FRONT AND LINING

HOOD AND LINING

BACK AND LINING

ZIP

08.
the hoody

The hoody is a jacket with a lining that fastens at the front with either a zip or buttons. It can be made with a big hood, with a collar, or with a simple, collarless neckline. It can be made with a coloured or patterned lining fabric to add a subtle splash of colour. It can be made cropped, to finish at the hips, or to hang below the bottom.

TECHNICAL VARIATIONS
the hoody can be made and worn in a variety of ways

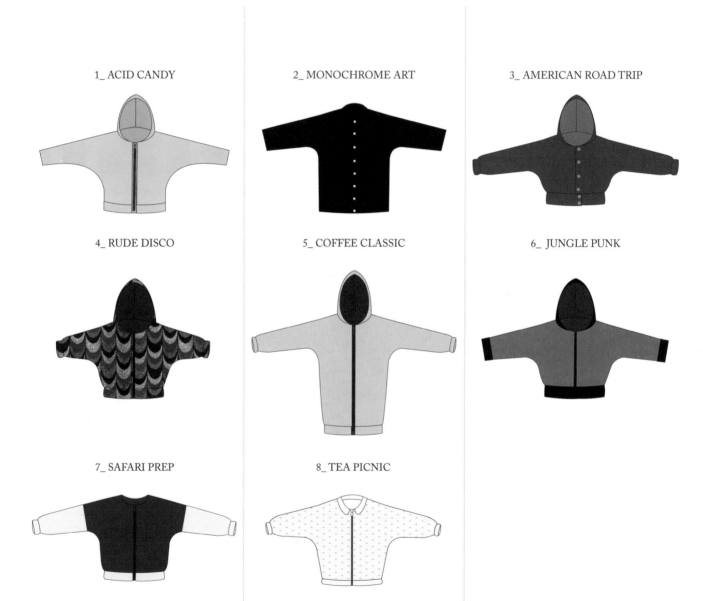

1_ ACID CANDY

2_ MONOCHROME ART

3_ AMERICAN ROAD TRIP

4_ RUDE DISCO

5_ COFFEE CLASSIC

6_ JUNGLE PUNK

7_ SAFARI PREP

8_ TEA PICNIC

1_ ACID CANDY

The Acid Candy hoody has been made using a fairly stiff medium-weight cotton and lined with a salmon-coloured fabric of similar weight and texture. The back piece is cut 56cm (22in) deep from shoulder to bottom. A 6cm (2½in)-deep waistband is attached, but no elastic is added at the wrist or waist of the hoody so that it has a clean, unbroken shape. The hood pieces measure 38cm (15in) from top to bottom along the straight vertical edge. The hoody fastens with a zip that has been sewn in so that it is mostly hidden.

2_ MONOCHROME ART

The Monochrome Art hoody is in fact more of a smart coat. It is made of wool suiting and is lined with a thick black polycotton. The back piece is cut 80cm (31½in) deep and the bottom edge of the coat hangs at the model's mid-thigh. No elastic has been added at either the sleeve ends or the bottom edge so the jacket retains a neat, clean shape. It has a collar that is 8cm (3¼in) deep and fastens with Velcro, and it has a row of decorative contrasting buttons.

3_ AMERICAN ROAD TRIP

The American Road Trip hoody has been made using a lightweight denim and is lined with a thick cotton. It has a tall hood that flops around the face. The hood pieces measure a long 45cm (17¾in) from top to bottom. The jacket itself is cropped, the back piece measuring 38cm (15in) deep. A 6cm (2½in)-deep waistband has been attached, through which elastic has been threaded. The hoody fastens with buttons.

4_ RUDE DISCO

The Rude Disco hoody is made with a light but stiff second-hand curtain fabric. It is lined with a thick black satin. The hoody has no additional waistband. Instead, the bottom of the hoody has been hemmed and elastic has been sewn directly to it. The elastic stretches across the back of the hoody so there is no gathered effect at the front. The hoody has very short sleeves with no elastic at the ends. It has an enormous hood and a wide neckline. The hood pieces were cut particularly tall, at 52cm (20½in).

5_ COFFEE CLASSIC

The Coffee Classic hoody is made with quite a thick fabric that does not wrinkle easily and needs steam ironing to form folds. The back piece is cut 79cm (31in) deep from shoulder to bottom, so that the bottom edge of the jacket hangs at mid-thigh. The sleeves have a deep hem with elastic pushed through to create shape. The waistband has also been threaded with thick elastic, just slightly smaller than the channels through which it has been pushed. The hoody has a maroon brushed cotton lining that matches the colour of the zip. It has a tall, 45cm (17¾in) hood that hangs around the face.

6_ JUNGLE PUNK

The Jungle Punk hoody is made using a thick wool-like fabric and lined with a heavy royal blue jersey. The back piece is 45cm (17¾in) deep from shoulder to bottom. A fairly thick 7cm (2¾in)-deep waistband in contrasting black has been added, and thick elastic pushed through it. Extra strips of fabric have been added at the ends of the sleeves. These are made in the same way as the waistband for the straight and skater skirts. The hood is 45cm (17¾in) tall, in contrasting black woollen fabric. The hoody fastens with a thick black zip.

7_ SAFARI PREP

The Safari Prep hoody has contrasting-colour sleeves and the feel of a vintage sports jacket. The initial back piece is 48cm (19in) deep and is cut with extremely shallow 'sleeves' ending just beyond the armpit. Rectangles of fabric are then added to create the sleeves. The hoody in fact has no hood or collar, but a neat simple neckline that has been cut fairly wide. A fairly thick 6cm (2½in) contrasting waistband has been added to the coat and a wide piece of elastic almost this deep has been pushed through it. The hoody fastens with a navy blue zip.

8_ TEA PICNIC

The Tea Picnic hoody is made of a soft printed polycotton and is lined with lightweight 100% cotton. The back piece is cut 56cm (22in) from shoulder to bottom, and the hoody has a 5cm (2in)-deep waistband added, through which elastic has been threaded. The sleeves are cropped just below the elbow, with elastic sewn directly to the fabric at the sleeve endings. This hoody has a 7cm (2¾in)-deep Peter Pan collar rather than a hood, and fastens with a clearly visible white zip.

First you are going to mark out and cut the back piece of your hoody. The hoody does not use set-in sleeves. The main body is made up of just three pieces: one back piece and two front pieces. You can use a jumper, jacket or hoody that you already own to cut these accurately. Find a jumper or shirt and put it on.

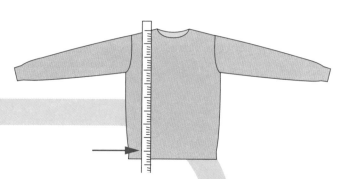

1_ Take your tape measure and put the zero end at the top shoulder seam of your jumper, at the neckline. Decide how long you would like your hoody to be and look at the measurement there. Write this number down. We'll call it your **depth measurement**.

If you plan to add a waistband at the bottom of your hoody, there is no need to add extra for seam allowance to this measurement. If you do not plan to add a waistband, add an extra 6cm (2½in) for seam allowance.

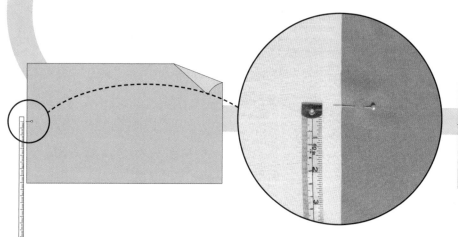

2_ Lay your fabric out and measure your depth measurement up the vertical edge.

3_ Put a pin in there.

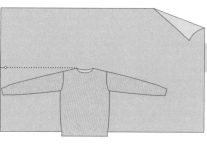

4_ Now take your jumper off. You need to lay it out on your fabric with the sleeves fully extended and the neck edge in line with your depth pin.

If you want to make a hoody with different-coloured sleeves, like the Safari Prep hoody, mark and cut very short sleeves at this point. You can then sew rectangles of another fabric to the sleeve ends to make them longer.

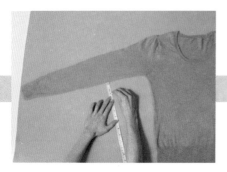

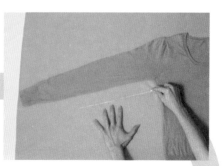

5_ If the garment you are using as a template fits you quite tightly along the sleeves, you will need to make your sleeves deeper. Measure an extra 5 or 6cm (2–2½in) downwards from your sleeve and make a mark with chalk. Do this in two or three places along the bottom edge of your sleeve.

6_ Draw a line under the left sleeve all the way to the armpit, joining up the marks you have made.

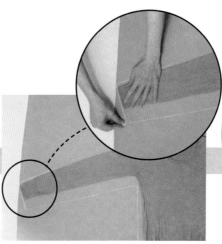

7_ Draw a vertical line downwards from your armpit point to the bottom of your fabric. Use your tape measure as a guide if you need to.

8_ Draw a line about 2cm (¾in) away from the upper edge of your sleeve, from the shoulder to the very end, and square off the end of your chalked sleeve with a short straight line following the end of your garment's sleeve.

9_ You need to round off the armpit area of your hoody with a curved line. Draw a curve that hits your sleeve line and vertical side line roughly in the middle of each.

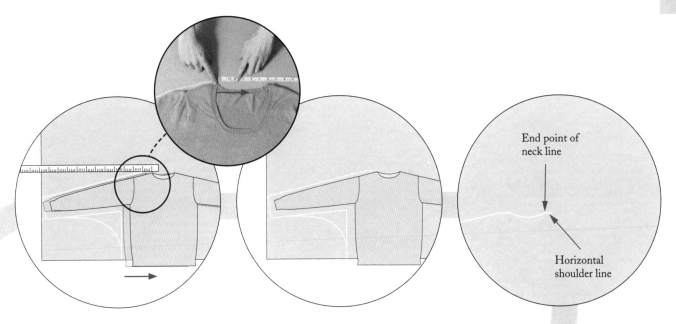

10_ Shift your garment to the right by about 5cm (2in).

11_ Continue your chalk shoulder line horizontally across for 5cm (2in). Then draw a curved neck shape, following the one on your garment.

12_ Make sure you clearly mark the end point of the neckline, where it changes angle as it meets the horizontal shoulder line. You can now put your garment to one side.

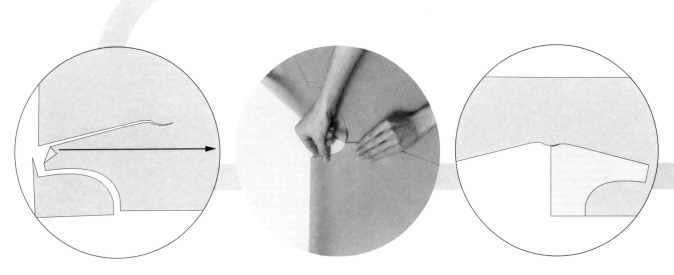

13_ Cut around the left half of the shape you have drawn. Then fold your cut half over to the right, matching up the neck corners.

14_ Use the folded half as a guide to help you cut the second half of your shape so that your back piece is symmetrical.

You will now use your back piece as a template to cut your two front pieces.

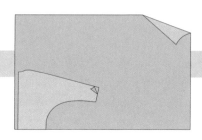

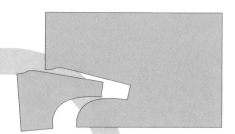

15_ With the piece still folded in half down the middle, lay it out on your fabric.

16_ Cut around this shape, adding an extra 3cm (1¼in) of width at the straight vertical folded edge. If you plan to fasten your hoody with buttons, or make a flap to cover your zip, add about 6cm (2½in) at each side so you can overlap the two pieces.

You need to make the neckline of this front piece lower so that it sits comfortably below your throat. You can make the neckline as deep as you like. The neckline of the hoody made here was deepened by 10cm (4in).

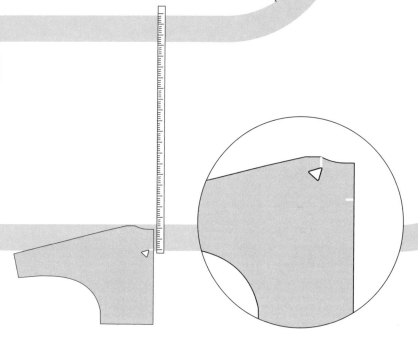

17_ Make a horizontal chalk mark where you want your neckline's lowest point to be, and a vertical mark running down from the edge of your neck line.

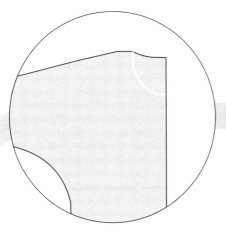

18_ Join these together with a curve and then cut along the line.

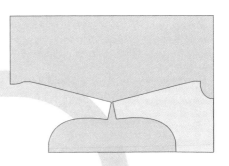

19_ Now take this front piece and flip it over so that you are looking at the wrong side of the fabric and lay it out on top of your fabric. Cut around this piece. You now have your back piece and two front pieces.

Use the pieces of fabric you have cut already to cut out exactly the same shapes from your lining fabric.

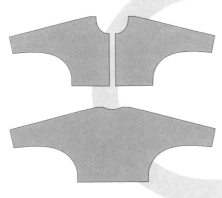

Now you are going to join your front pieces to your back piece.

20_ Lay your back piece out with the right side of the fabric facing upwards. Take one front piece and lay it on top of your back piece with the right side of the fabric facing downwards. The right sides should be touching each other.

21_ Pin the pieces together all the way along the shoulder edge, along the under edge of the sleeve and down the side, then sew along these pinned edges with straight stitch, about 1.5cm (⅝in) from the edge.

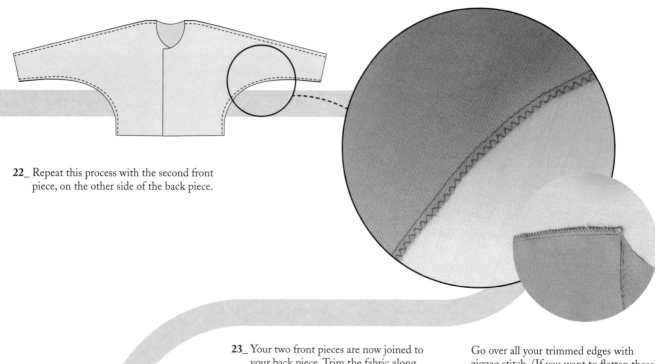

22_ Repeat this process with the second front piece, on the other side of the back piece.

23_ Your two front pieces are now joined to your back piece. Trim the fabric along all the joins so there is just 4 or 5mm (³⁄₁₆in–¼in) beyond your rows of stitching. Your hoody will hang comfortably if you can do this at the curved underarm areas.

Go over all your trimmed edges with zigzag stitch. (If you want to flatten these seams, push them to one side and stitch them down, as explained in the Grecian dress instructions on page 56.)

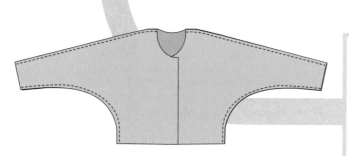

24_ Repeat these steps with your lining pieces.

If you want to add pockets to your hoody, like the Safari Prep hoody on page 147, now is the time to do it. See pages 16–17 for guidance on this. If you would like to make a collar rather than a hood, see pages 102–106 in the cloak instructions.

Now it is time to make your hood.

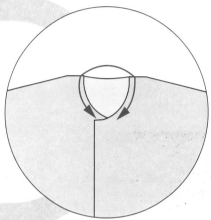

25_ Before you start marking your shapes, get a ball of string or thread and cut a piece that is the same distance as the distance around the neck edge of your hoody.

Get a hoody (or a jacket that has a hood), unfasten it and fold it in half down the centre, so the hood is folded in half vertically. You are going to use this as a template.

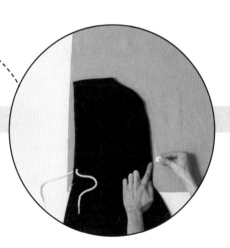

26_ Lay your hoody out on your fabric with the straight front line of the hood running parallel with the straight vertical edge of your fabric. You need to draw around the outer curve of your hood with tailor's chalk.

27_ Start with a straight line at the vertical back edge of your hood.

28_ If the garment you are using as a guide is made of jersey or stretch fabric and has a snug-fitting hood, you need to make your hood taller so that it will fit over your head. Draw a horizontal line at the top of your hood that is about 10cm (4in) above the top of your garment.

29_ Join these straight lines with a curve.

30_ The bottom of your hood needs to form a sort of gentle, stretched S-shape. At the bottom of your hood, draw a straight horizontal line inwards from the back…

31_ … and from the front.

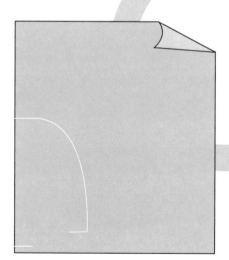
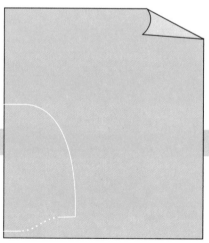

32_ You can remove your guiding garment now. If the width of your hood were divided into quarters, each of these horizontal lines should cover about one-quarter of the distance across your hood.

33_ Join your two horizontal lines with a sloping line to mark your sloping S-shape.

34_ The shape you have drawn will form half of your hood. Take your piece of string and fold it in half. Lay it out so that it runs along the stretched 'S' at the bottom of your hood.

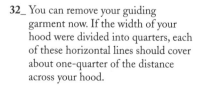

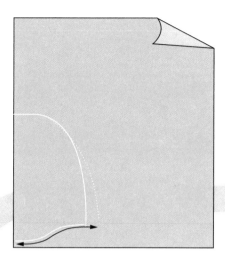

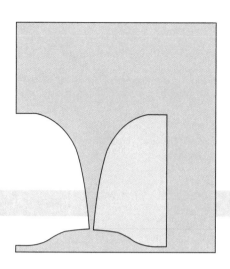

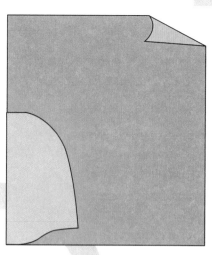

35_ If your string is longer than the line you have drawn, extend the line at the back so that it is the same length as your folded string.

36_ Cut out your first hood piece, then flip it over and use it as a template to cut a mirror image of it from your main fabric.

37_ Then use one piece as a template to cut two pieces from your lining fabric.

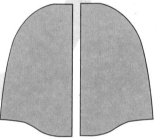

38_ Make sure you cut two pieces that mirror each other, rather than two identical pieces.

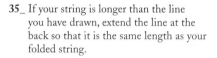

Next, you need to join your hood pieces together in pairs.

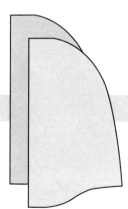

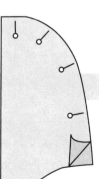

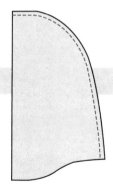

39_ Lay one of your outer pieces out flat with the right side of the fabric facing upwards, then lay the other piece face down on top of it.

40_ Pin all the way along the long curved edge that will form the 'backbone' of your hood. Sew along this line with straight stitch.

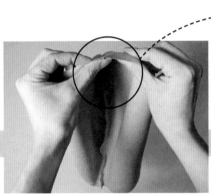

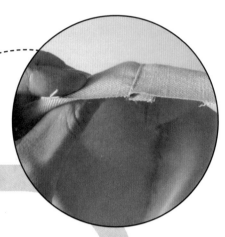

41_ Turn your hood the right way around so that the neat edge of your seam is on the outside. Push the flaps of your seam to one side and sew them flat, to make a nice neat join.

42_ With the right side of your hood facing upwards, sew a line of straight stitch close to the seam (a millimetre or two away). Your stitches should catch the flap of fabric on the inside of your hood. This row of stitches flattens the seam and neatens your hood.

Now you need to join the lining and outer pieces of your hood.

43_ Repeat steps 39 to 42 with your lining pieces.

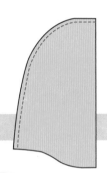

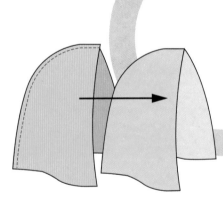

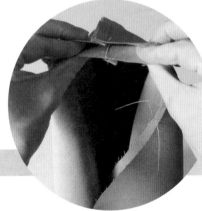

44_ Turn your lining so that you are looking at the wrong side of the fabric. Take your outer piece and insert it inside your lining piece so that the right sides of both pieces are touching each other.

45_ Line up the central seams of the two pieces so they sit exactly on top of one another.

46_ You are going to attach the two pieces by sewing them together along the raw edges at the front of your hood. Pin the two together, starting at the central seam, and continue pinning all along this edge.

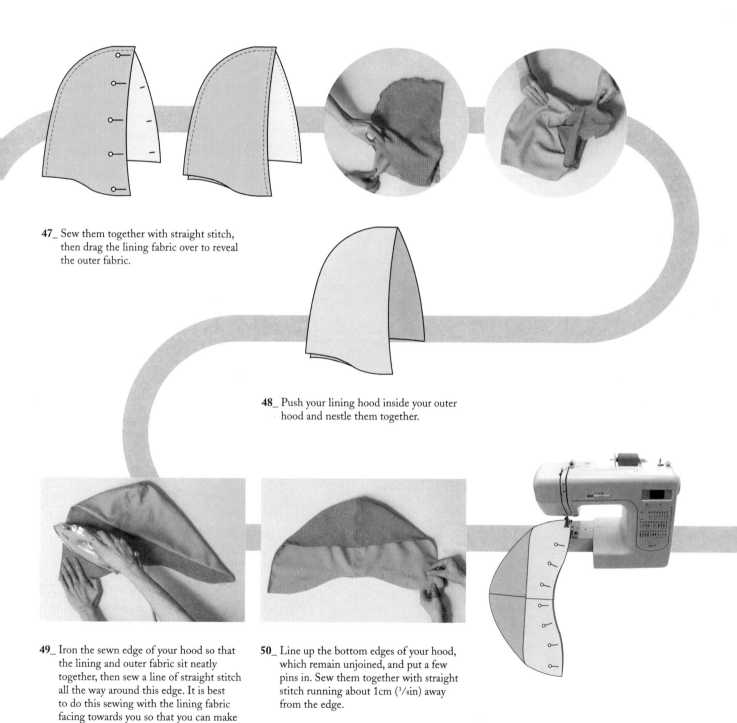

47_ Sew them together with straight stitch, then drag the lining fabric over to reveal the outer fabric.

48_ Push your lining hood inside your outer hood and nestle them together.

49_ Iron the sewn edge of your hood so that the lining and outer fabric sit neatly together, then sew a line of straight stitch all the way around this edge. It is best to do this sewing with the lining fabric facing towards you so that you can make sure it is not hanging over the outer fabric. Your bobbin thread will show on the outside of your hood, so make sure it matches your outer fabric.

50_ Line up the bottom edges of your hood, which remain unjoined, and put a few pins in. Sew them together with straight stitch running about 1cm (³/₈in) away from the edge.

Now you need to attach your hood to your body pieces. You are going to pin your hood into your lining piece, with the lining of your hood touching the right side of your lining fabric.

51_ Start with your lining piece turned inside out.

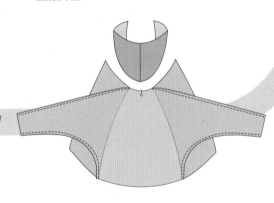

52_ Find the centre of the back of your neckline by folding that area in half (making the two shoulder seams meet) and put a pin in to mark the spot.

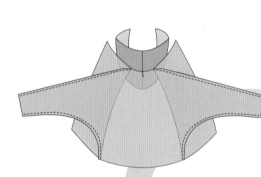

53_ Position the central seam of your hood here.

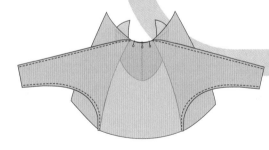

54_ Pin it to your lining piece, with the bottom edge of your hood matching the neck edge of your lining piece.

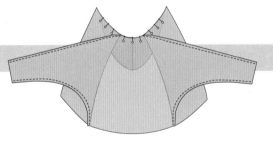

55_ Continue pinning the entire bottom edge of your hood to the neck edge. Insert your pins at right angles to the edge, closer to the edge than you normally would so the end of the pin hangs over. This will give you the best chance of sewing your hood in wrinkle-free.

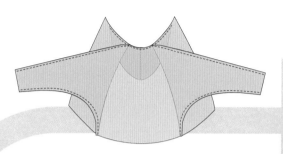

56_ Sew your hood to your lining piece along this pinned edge.

Now turn to the outer part of your hoody. Turn it the right way round.

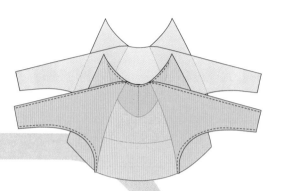

57_ Push each sleeve of your outer hoody down into the sleeve of your lining. When you have nestled the two together, you should be looking at the wrong sides of your fabrics all over and your hood should be completely hidden from view.

58_ Match up the shoulder seams of your outer fabric with the shoulder seams of your lining fabric and pin your outer piece to your lining piece along the neckline. Your pins should go through the outer fabric, the hood, and the lining. Continue pinning all the way down your two front vertical edges, then sew along these edges with straight stitch.

If you feel unsure about sewing directly over the pins, roughly hand-sew along the pinned neck edge before machining, removing your pins as you go.

59_ Trim the fabric at your collar so there is just 3 or 4mm ($^1/_8$–$^3/_{16}$in) beyond your row of stitching. Trim the top corners of your vertical edges.

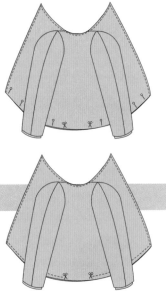

Now turn your hoody the right way around so that the hood emerges. Push the sleeves of lining fabric inside the sleeves of your hoody and arrange the two pieces until they are sitting comfortably inside one another.

60_ If you are not adding a waistband, you can sew along the bottom of your hoody now. Make sure you leave a gap of about 20cm (8in) so that you can reach in and pull it the right way around.

61_ Pull out the fabric at the corners, then go over the straight edges with an iron.

Now you can make a waistband for the bottom of your hoody. You can do this to make it longer, for visual effect (by using a different colour fabric) or to create a tunnel into which you can insert elastic.

You can make your waistband continue past the front edges of your hoody so there is some overlap, as in the American Road Trip hoody. If you want to do this, cut your waistband strip even longer.

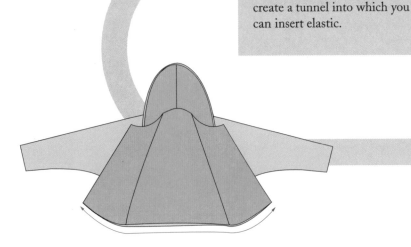

62_ Measure the full length of the bottom edge of your hoody and add an additional 5cm (2in). Cut a strip of fabric this wide and double the depth of the waistband you wish to make, plus an additional 3cm (1¼in).

You are going to make and attach a waistband in the same way as the waistband on the straight skirt (see page 43).

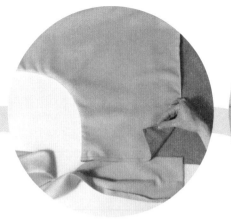
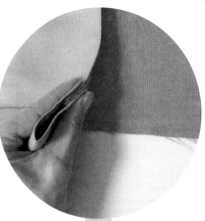

63_ As for the skirt waistband, iron a flap of fabric under along both long edges, then iron the full strip in half. Hem one short end of your waistband piece and position it so that it is lined up with one vertical front edge of your hoody.

64_ The edge of your hoody should be sandwiched between the front and back of your waistband.

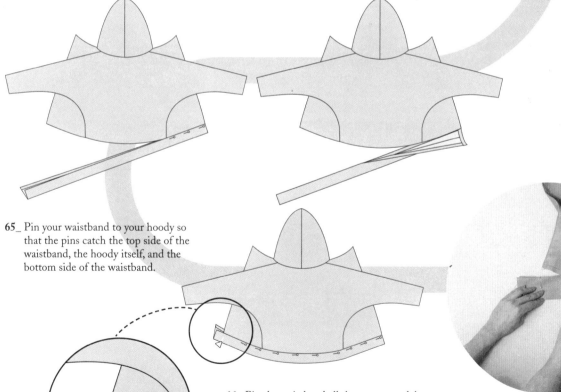

65_ Pin your waistband to your hoody so that the pins catch the top side of the waistband, the hoody itself, and the bottom side of the waistband.

66_ Pin the waistband all the way around, but stop about 10cm (4in) short of the other side. You need to make your waistband just the right length now. Put a pin into your waistband fabric, or make a mark with chalk, to mark the point where you would like it to end.

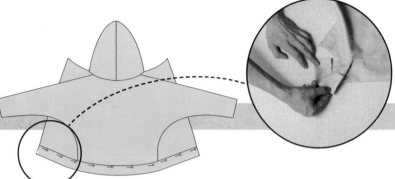

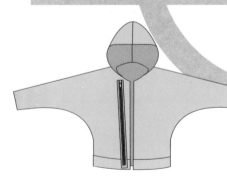

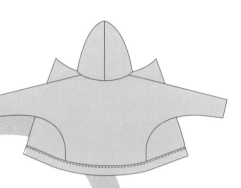

67_ Fold the end of your waistband in on itself so that it is the right length.

68_ Now sew your waistband to your hoody with a line of straight stitch running all the way from one side to the other.

If you want to add elastic to the waistband of your hoody so that it pinches in to your body and wrinkles up at the bottom, now is the time to do so. Push your strip of elastic through the waistband using a safety pin, as shown in the trouser instructions (see page 183). When the loose end has just disappeared into the waistband, pin it down and sew over it with a short line of straight stitch so it is anchored into place. Keep pulling your elastic round; when it is the right length, hide the end just inside the waistband and sew it down with straight stitch too.

Now you need to add a zip to the front of your hoody. Make sure you buy a zip that is open-ended.

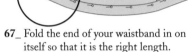

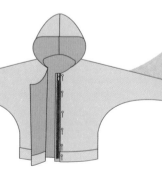

69_ Slide the zip under one of the finished front edges of your hoody.

70_ Pin this side of the zip to your hoody.

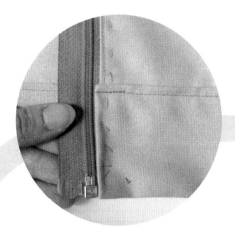

71_ Roughly hand-stitch it into place with long stitches that will be easy to unpick.

72_ Position the second side of your hoody over the other edge of the zip.

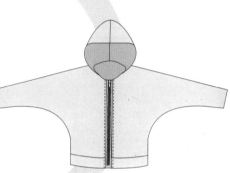

Finish your sleeve ends either by hemming the ends or adding an extra strip of fabric (with elastic if you choose) in the same way you added the waistband. You can also make a deep hem, which can be threaded with elastic in the same way the waistband on the trousers is threaded on pages 182–184.

73_ Put your zip foot onto your sewing machine and sew along each edge with a row of straight stitch. See the straight skirt instructions on pages 38–40 for a more detailed look at sewing in a zip.

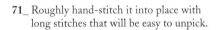

you have made a hoody

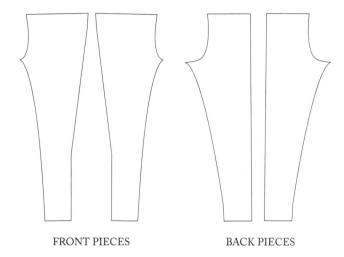

FRONT PIECES   BACK PIECES

09.

the trousers

These trousers are simple and versatile, with tucks at the front and no fastening. They are gathered at the top by a strip of elastic that can hug the waist for an elegant appearance or cling to the hips for a more casual look. The trousers are made up of four pieces of fabric: two pieces form the front of the trousers, and two form the back.

TECHNICAL VARIATIONS
the trousers can be made and worn in a variety of ways

1_ ACID CANDY

2_ MONOCHROME ART

3_ AMERICAN ROAD TRIP

4_ RUDE DISCO

5_ COFFEE CLASSIC

6_ JUNGLE PUNK

7_ SAFARI PREP

8_ TEA PICNIC

1_ ACID CANDY

The Acid Candy trousers are made using quite a tough, medium-weight fabric. They are made with two tucks on either side at the front and pinch the waist with a 4cm (1½in)-deep waistband, through which elastic has been threaded. The trousers are fairly loose-fitting. They are peg leg-style trousers, sloping in towards the ankles.

2_ MONOCHROME ART

The Monochrome Art trousers are made with a floppy suiting fabric. They sit on the hips and have a boyish feel. The trousers have three pleats on each side, each using about 3cm (1¼in) of fabric. The pleats have been made to sit near the outer edge of the trousers. The top edge of the trousers has been hemmed and two elongated white belt loops have been added. A belt draws the trousers in at the waist.

3_ AMERICAN ROAD TRIP

The American Road Trip trousers are made from a fairly thin fabric that is nevertheless quite tough. It has an Aztec-style print. The trousers are made with no tucks at all. The shape is simply created by threading a skinny piece of elastic through a 1.5cm (⅝in)-deep waistband. The trousers do not taper in towards the ankle; they are even in width all the way down to create a comfortable, baggy appearance.

4_ RUDE DISCO

The Rude Disco trousers are made using a very thin, almost transparent blackish-gold fabric. The trousers have two pleats on either side at the front, each using 5cm (2in) of fabric. A fairly deep 5.5cm (2¼in) piece of elastic has been threaded through the 6cm (2½in) waistband. The trousers sit on the hips. They are fairly baggy at the top with a low crotch, but are so slim at the bottom that they grip the calves. A slight stretch in the fabric allows for this.

5_ COFFEE CLASSIC

The Coffee Classic trousers are made with quite a thick neutral-coloured fabric that does not crease easily. There are two tucks on each side of the trousers, each using 5cm (2in) of fabric. These have been ironed to hold their shape. The tucks sit below the waistband, creating a flared effect at the top of the trousers. The trousers are held up by a belt rather than with elastic. They are cropped so that they finish above the ankle.

6_ JUNGLE PUNK

The Jungle Punk trousers are made with a printed cotton that is fairly stiff. No additional fabric for tucks is added when these trousers are cut, so they have a fairly slim fit all the way down. A piece of elastic 4.5cm (1¾in) deep is sewn directly to the trousers, as explained in the Grecian dress instructions (see pages 57–59).

7_ SAFARI PREP

The Safari Prep trousers are made from a tough cotton with a bold printed pattern. They have been made as shorts. They have one pleat on each side at the front, sitting near the outer edge of the garment. Each pleat uses 5cm (2in) of fabric. No waistband is created for the trousers – the top edge is simply hemmed. A 2.5cm (1in)-deep piece of elastic is sewn directly to the trousers just below the top edge.

8_ TEA PICNIC

The Tea Picnic trousers are also shorts. They are made using a very thin polycotton. There are no tucks at the top. Instead, the shorts are brought in at the waist by six rows of shirring. (For guidance on shirring, see the DIYcouture website, www.diy-couture.co.uk.) The shirring finishes below the top edge of the trousers, creating a flared shape. The shorts have a scalloped bottom edge created by adding a partial lining, as with the Tea Picnic straight skirt.

First you are going to mark and cut one front piece for your trousers. The shape you are aiming for is similar to that of a straight-cut pair of jeans when they are folded in half, but flares from the knee outwards up to the waist. Remember that as long as you make something like this shape, you will be able to make a good pair of trousers. Try not to become too fixated on the measurements; they are there to offer guidance.

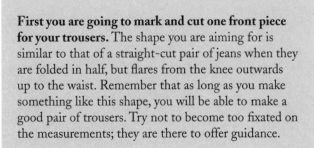

1_ Get a pair of trousers that fit you well around the hips and are the right length. Your favourite pair of jeans will work perfectly. You are going to use these as a guide to mark out the shape of your first front piece.

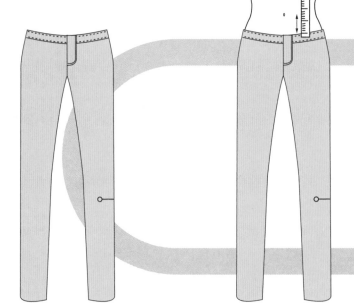

2_ Put your trousers on and stick a pin into them at knee level.

3_ With the trousers still on, measure from the waistband upwards to your actual waist (the thinnest bit of you around the middle). Write this measurement down. We will call this your **hip–waist measurement**.

4_ Now take the trousers off, fold them in half, and lay them on your fabric. Lay them so that the bottom of the trousers sits at the bottom edge of your fabric and the vertical edge of your trousers sits 2 or 3cm (¾–1¼in) inland. This is your seam allowance.

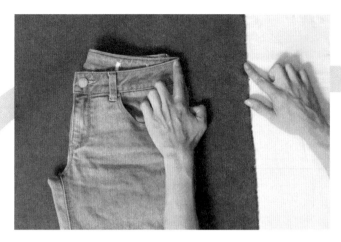

Some of the trousers shown in the book have no tucks made in them. The Tea Picnic shorts and American Road Trip wide-leg trousers have no tucks; however, the same extra fabric added here was also added to those garments. This gives them a slightly loose shape at the top. The Jungle Punk trousers had no extra fabric added for tucks. They were simply marked out by drawing around a pair of jeans with 4cm (1½in) extra all the way round. The trousers are a bit of a squeeze to get into, as they fit much more tightly all over.

5_ The trousers need to sit inland even more to allow room for tucks. You need to decide now how big you would like your tucks to be. Use the variations on pages 170–171 to help you. The Acid Candy trousers made here have two tucks on each side. Each tuck uses 4cm (1½in) of fabric. Therefore, the guide trousers used are moved 8cm (3¼in) in from where they were positioned.

If your guide trousers are hipsters and you want to make high-waisted trousers instead, you need to add extra length at the top of your trouser shape.

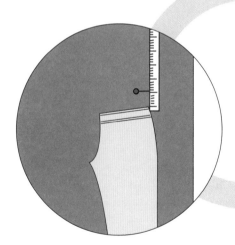

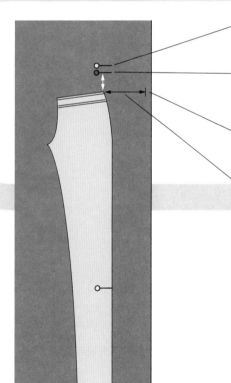

The **waistband pin** sits above the red pin, marking *double* the amount of fabric that will be folded over to make the waistband.

Your hip–waist measurement, shown by the white arrow, is measured upwards from the top of your hipster trousers and marked by the **hip-waist pin**.

Seam allowance: Before the trousers were shifted inland to allow for tucks they sat here, 2 or 3cm (¾–1¼in) from the edge.

Tuck allowance: The black arrow marks the distance the trousers have been moved to allow for tucks.

6_ Measure your hip–waist measurement upwards from the top edge of your guide trousers. Put a pin in to mark this measurement. This is shown with a red pin on the diagrams. We'll call it the hip–waist pin.

7_ You need to add extra length to allow for a folded top edge that will contain your elastic later on. Measure the depth of your elastic, double it and add 1.5cm (⁵⁄₈in). We'll call this your **waistband measurement**. Measure this distance upwards from the pin you just inserted and put another pin in there. We will call this your waistband pin. It is shown in yellow on the diagram.

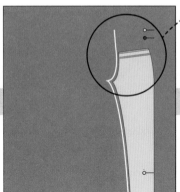

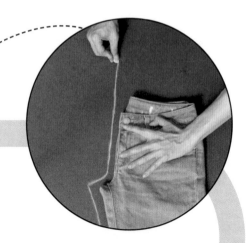

8_ Draw around the inner leg and crotch seam of your guide trousers with tailor's chalk. The trousers you are making need to be slightly wider than a pair of trousers with a zip fastening, which allows access for your bottom and hips. The trousers need to be loose enough to go over your bottom and hips. When you draw around your trouser shape, draw your chalk lines 3 or 4cm (1¼–1½in) away from your actual trousers to allow for this.

9_ Continue drawing your crotch seam line all the way up until it is level with your waistband pin.

10_ Now draw a horizontal straight line to the very edge of your fabric.

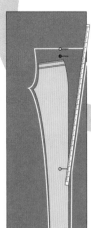

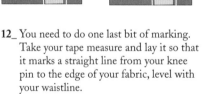

11_ Next, draw upwards from the bottom point of your trousers, stopping when you reach your knee pin.

12_ You need to do one last bit of marking. Take your tape measure and lay it so that it marks a straight line from your knee pin to the edge of your fabric, level with your waistline.

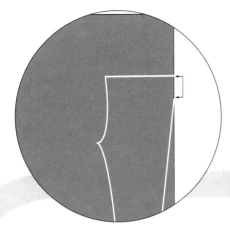

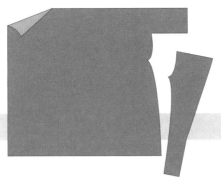

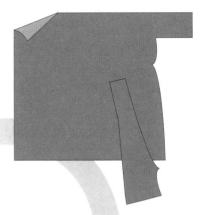

13_ Use the tape measure as a guide to draw a diagonal line here with your tailor's chalk. Make your chalk mark below your tape measure, so it hits the edge of your fabric below your waistline, leaving a stretch of vertical edge. This needs to be at least double the depth you intend your waistband to be (marked by the black bracket in the diagram).

14_ Now all your measuring and marking is complete, so you can cut out your first front trouser piece.

15_ You will need to cut another piece exactly the same shape to make the other front half, but to make the best use of your fabric, cut out one of your back pieces first. Swivel your first piece around so that the foot end is now pointing away from you.

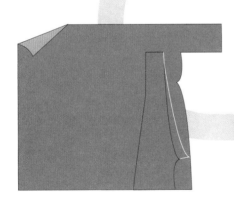

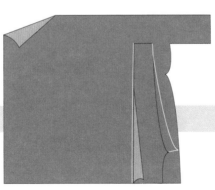

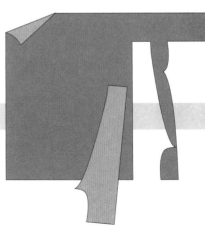

16_ The back piece needs a bit of extra fabric at the crotch area to allow your bottom some space in the trousers. Measure an extra 10cm (4in) horizontally across from your crotch point. Mark this with chalk and draw a line from the new crotch point to the ankle.

17_ You do not need to include the extra fabric you added for tucks on your front trouser piece. You can simply fold in this flap of fabric and draw a line with your tailor's chalk while it is folded. Cut out.

18_ You now have one front and one back piece. You need to cut a mirror image of each one. Flip the back piece that you have just cut and use it as a template to cut your second back piece.

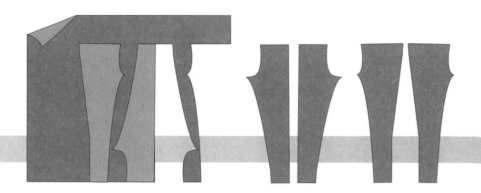

19_ Then take your original front piece, flip it over and use that as a template to cut a second front piece.

20_ You have now cut the four pieces of fabric that make up your trousers. Zigzag-stitch along the curved edge and down the inner leg line of all four of your pieces now.

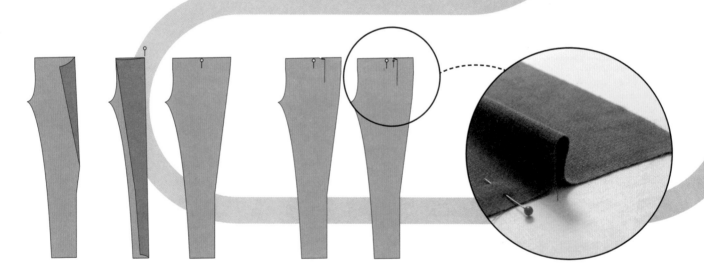

21_ Lay out one of your front pieces with the wrong side of the fabric facing upwards. To help you place the tucks evenly, fold the top of your piece in half to find the centre point and put a pin in there.

22_ Open the top out again. You can now space your tucks evenly on either side of your central pin. Nip a bit of fabric between your fingers on one side of the pin and continue nipping it so you form an even ridge running about 15cm (6in) downwards from the waistline.

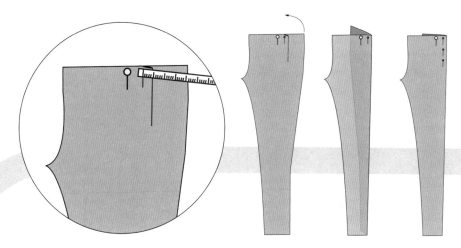

23_ Pin this ridge at the top and use your tape measure or a ruler to check that it uses the amount of fabric that you planned to use.

24_ Continue pinning the ridge about 10cm (4in) vertically downwards from your waistline.

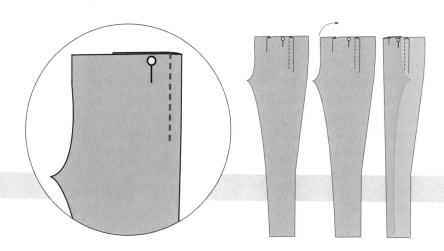

25_ You need to secure this ridge with lines of straight stitch running vertically down your trouser leg. Choose a long straight stitch that can be unpicked easily. When you reach the bottom of your pinned line, do not run your machine back and forth to secure the stitching. You need to make it as easy as possible to unpick these stitches later.

26_ Repeat this process on the other side of your centre pin, for as many tucks as you had planned.

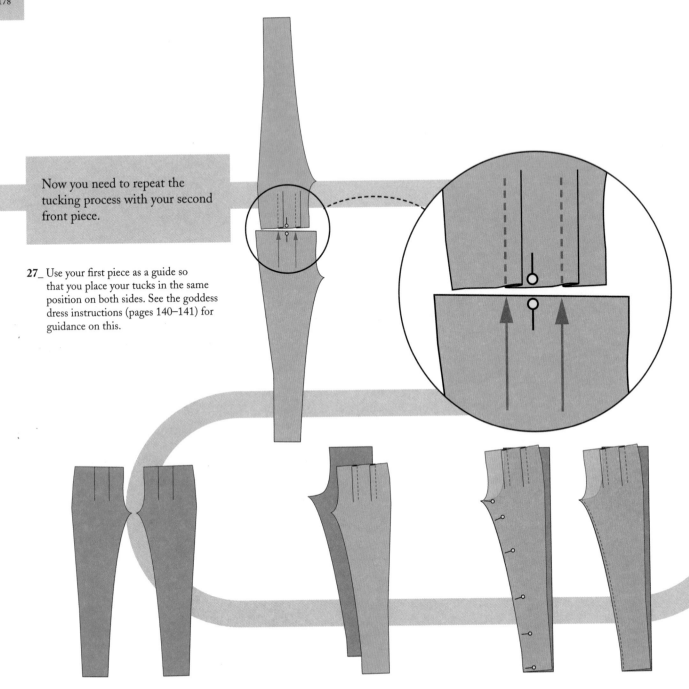

Now you need to repeat the tucking process with your second front piece.

27_ Use your first piece as a guide so that you place your tucks in the same position on both sides. See the goddess dress instructions (pages 140–141) for guidance on this.

28_ You now have two neatly tucked front trouser pieces.

29_ Lay out one of your back pieces with the right side facing upwards, then lay the corresponding front piece on top of it with the right side facing downwards – the right sides should be touching each other.

30_ Match the pieces up and pin them together along the inner leg edge, then join them together with a line of straight stitch running along this edge.

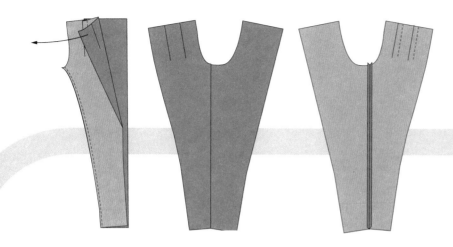

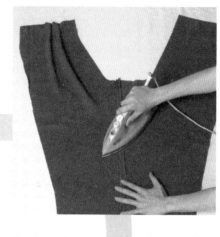

31_ Open your trouser piece out, then flip it over so you are looking at the wrong side of the fabric.

Repeat this process with your other two pieces, joining them together down the inside leg edge to form one side of your trousers. You now have two separate sides to your trousers and you are going to join them together.

32_ Open the seam with your fingers as if you are opening a book and iron the flaps down as flat as you can so that they sit against the fabric.

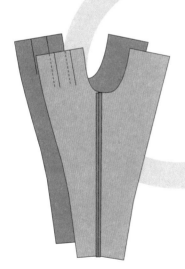

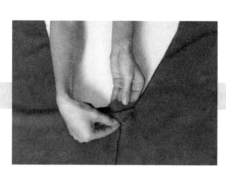

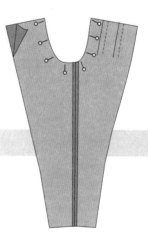

33_ Lay out one piece with the right side facing upwards and then lay the other piece on top of it facing downwards. You should be looking at the wrong side of your fabric.

34_ Match them up around the crotch area, which will form a U-shape. Try to match up the crotch seams as precisely as possible; this will help your trousers to hang well.

35_ Pin all the way around this curved line, then sew it with straight stitch.

36_ Now you need to sew up the outer edges of the trousers. Reposition your trousers and line these edges up as shown. Pin them into place. Your trousers won't sit exactly flat, as your back pieces are bigger than your front pieces. Don't worry about this – you are not flat either. If some of your trouser pieces are longer than others, just make sure you match the pieces at the tops. You can trim the bottoms as necessary.

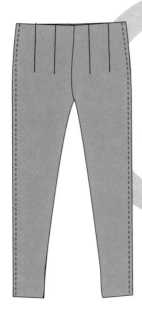

37_ Sew up each side with a line of straight stitch.

Your trousers are now really taking shape. Try them on inside out to see how they are fitting.

If the trousers are baggier than you would like, take them off and sew up each side a little bit further in. Trim off any excess fabric and unpick the stitches from your first line of straight stitch.

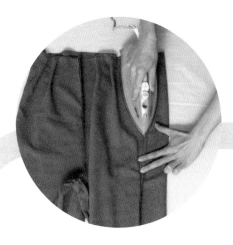

You are now going to fold over the top edge of your trousers to make a tunnel, through which you will thread elastic.

You can choose to sew a piece of elastic directly on to the fabric at the waist edge of your trousers; this flattens the fabric slightly more. The Jungle Punk and Safari Prep trousers have been finished like this. For guidance on this, see the Grecian dress instructions on pages 58–59. The Tea Picnic shorts have also not had elastic threaded through them; they were hemmed at the top and shirred. For guidance on shirring, see the DIYcouture website (www.diy-couture.co.uk).

38_ When you have fitted your trousers, open the side seams and iron them so that they sit flat. To make long-lasting trousers, zigzag-stitch up all four of the long seam edges so they do not fray.

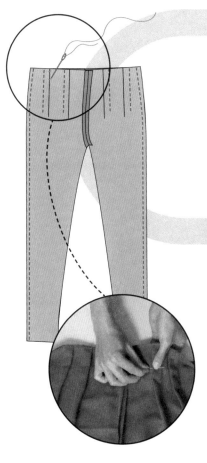

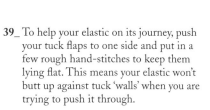

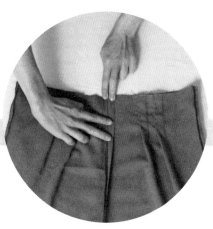

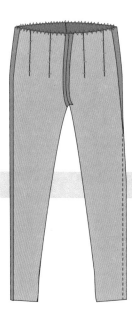

39_ To help your elastic on its journey, push your tuck flaps to one side and put in a few rough hand-stitches to keep them lying flat. This means your elastic won't butt up against tuck 'walls' when you are trying to push it through.

40_ With your trousers still inside out, make sure the flaps at the side seams and at the front and back are sitting open, then zigzag all the way around the top waist edge of your trousers, sewing these seam flaps open.

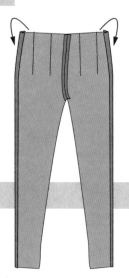

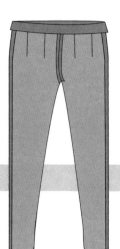

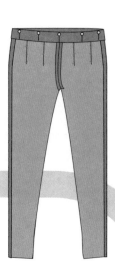

41_ Fold the top edge of your trousers over, making sure the fold is deeper than your elastic.

42_ Pin this fold into place, with your pins at right angles to the edge of the fabric.

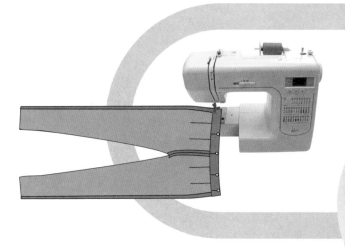

43_ Then sew it down with a line of straight stitch running close to the zigzagged edge of the fold. Stop your row of stitching about 6cm (2½in) before you get back to where you started. You need this gap in order to insert your elastic into the tunnel you have just created.

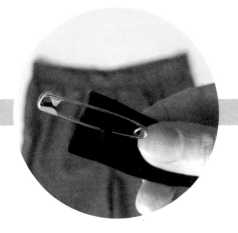

44_ Take your elastic and cut a piece that is slightly shorter than the distance around your waist – hold it around yourself to get the right length. Stick a safety pin into the end of your strip of elastic. This will help you push the elastic through, as it will nose its way through the tunnel.

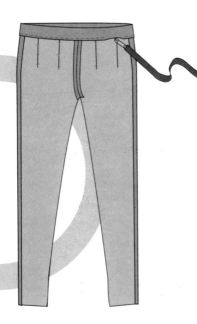

45_ Push your elastic into your waistband tunnel and work it around with your fingers until just the last tip of the elastic is visible.

46_ Put a pin through your waistband and elastic to keep this end from slipping into the tunnel and disappearing.

47_ Now continue to pull your safety-pinned end around the tunnel until it pops out at the hole where you began.

48_ Pin the two ends of the elastic together, making sure the elastic isn't twisted.

49_ Sew the two ends of elastic together with a line of straight stitch. Trim them very close to this line, then go over the ends with zigzag stitch.

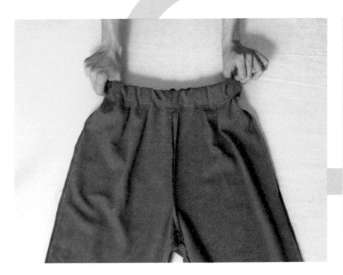
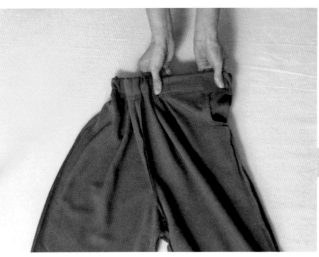

50_ Stretch the waistband of your trousers so that your elastic ends disappear into the tunnel.

51_ To finish the waistband, you just need to sew a short row of straight stitch to seal the gap you left and close in your elastic. You can now unpick the stitches that are holding the tucks in place.

To make a scalloped edge for the Tea Picnic trousers or straight skirt you need to attach and shape a border of fabric.

a_ Cut a fabric border to the size of the front and back pieces of your skirt or trousers.

b_ Lay right sides together, pin, and draw a wavy edge with tailor's chalk along the bottom edge.

c_ Sew just inside the chalk line.

d_ Cut away the excess fabric.

e_ Turn your garment inside out and iron carefully.

f_ Hand-sew the side and top edges together so the stitching cannot be seen on the outside.

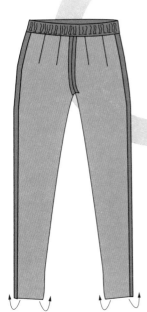 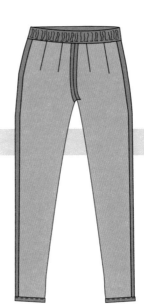

you have made a pair of trousers

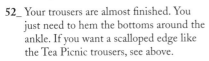

52_ Your trousers are almost finished. You just need to hem the bottoms around the ankle. If you want a scalloped edge like the Tea Picnic trousers, see above.

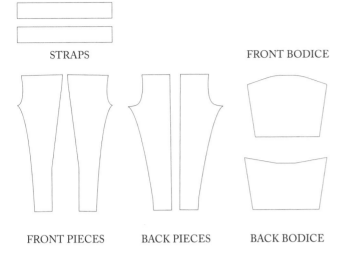

STRAPS

FRONT BODICE

FRONT PIECES

BACK PIECES

BACK BODICE

10.

the romper

The romper builds on the trousers with a shaped bodice to create a flattering one-piece. The bodice is made with a front piece, a back piece and two strips of fabric to form a facing through which elastic can be threaded. It can be made with or without straps.

TECHNICAL VARIATIONS

the romper can be made and worn in a variety of ways

1_ ACID CANDY

2_ MONOCHROME ART

3_ AMERICAN ROAD TRIP

4_ RUDE DISCO

5_ COFFEE CLASSIC

6_ JUNGLE PUNK

7_ SAFARI PREP

8_ TEA PICNIC

1_ ACID CANDY

The Acid Candy romper is made with a floppy synthetic fabric. The trousers are full-length and tapered at the ankle. They have two tucks on each side at the front, each using about 4cm (1½in) of fabric. The bodice is a fairly long 43cm (17in) and flops over at the bottom. The romper is brought in at the waist by a band of elastic 3.5cm (1⅜in) deep. The facing at the top of the bodice is cut 5cm (2in) deep, and has been sewn to form a channel 3cm (1¼in) deep, through which a thin piece of elastic is threaded. The romper has two thick straps. Each finished strap measures 6cm (2½in) across.

2_ MONOCHROME ART

The Monochrome Art romper has been made with a tough white fabric, almost like canvas. The trousers flare gently, and the bottoms are turned up to look like culottes. They have two pleats on each side at the front, each using about 4cm (1½in) of fabric. The bodice is 34cm (13½in) long and the model has pulled the waistband down to sit on her hips. The waistband is 4cm (1½in) deep and is threaded with elastic just slightly narrower than this. The facing at the top of the bodice is threaded with the same elastic. The romper is finished with two 9cm (3½in)-wide straps in contrasting black.

3_ AMERICAN ROAD TRIP

The American Road Trip romper is made with a fairly thin, floppy printed cotton. The trousers are full-length with a wide leg. They have four slim tucks at the front on each side, each using 2cm (¾in) of fabric. The bodice is 38cm (15in) long, and there is some overhang at the waist. The facing at the top of the bodice is cut 2.5cm (1in) deep, and sewn to form a channel 1.5cm (⅝in) deep, through which thin elastic is threaded. The romper has two straps, 3.5cm (1⅜in) across.

4_ RUDE DISCO

The Rude Disco romper is made with a thin gold fabric. The trousers have been made as short shorts, with no tucks added. The bodice is a fairly short 28cm (11in), so there is only a little overhang at the waist. Instead of a waistband, a 4cm (1½in)-deep strip of elastic is sewn directly to the romper at the waist. The facing at the top of the bodice creates a tunnel 3.5cm (1⅜in) deep; a strip of elastic 3cm (1¼in) deep has been pushed through this. This romper is strapless.

5_ COFFEE CLASSIC

The Coffee Classic romper is made with crêpe-effect fabric. The cropped trousers have two tucks on each side at the front, each taking 2.5cm (1in) of fabric. The bodice is a fairly long 43cm (17in) and flops over, almost covering the waist. The waist is brought in by a belt. The facing at the top of the bodice is narrow, at just 2.5cm (1in), and a skinny piece of 4mm (³⁄₁₆in)-wide elastic is threaded through it. The romper is finished with two pieces of velveteen ribbon sewn to the centre of the bodice. These tie in a bow at the neck.

6_ JUNGLE PUNK

The Jungle Punk romper is made from a floppy tangerine fabric that has a slight stretch. The trousers are cropped below the knee for a playful feel. The bodice is 32cm (12½in) long. The romper is cinched at the waist with a thick strip of elastic. The facing at the top of the bodice has an extra line of stitching about 1.5cm (⅝in) below the edge. This creates an almost frilled effect, as elastic has been threaded below it. The romper has no straps, and two large pockets on the hips.

7_ SAFARI PREP

The Safari Prep romper is made from a thin, printed fabric. It is a hybrid of the trousers and the goddess dress. The trousers taper at the ankles. They have two pleats on each side at the front, each one using about 4cm (1½in) of fabric. They have a deep 5cm (2in) hem at the top, through which elastic has been threaded. Before the elastic was pushed through, a goddess dress-style bust piece was sewn to the front of the trousers. This bust piece, cut 32cm (12½in) wide, is sewn so that it overlaps in the middle, completely covering the chest area.

8_ TEA PICNIC

The Tea Picnic romper is made with thin printed polycotton. The trousers are full-length and have two tucks on each side at the front, each using 5cm (2in) of fabric. The bodice is short, measuring just 26cm (10¼in) from top to bottom. The romper has a 3cm (1¼in)-deep waistband and elastic just thinner than this has been pushed through. The tunnel made by the facing at the top edge of the bodice is just 2cm (¾in) deep, with a skinny piece of elastic threaded through it. Six decorative buttons are sewn to the front of the bodice, and ribbons are attached at front and back, to tie at the shoulder.

To begin with, you need to cut and join the trouser pieces in exactly same way as in the trouser instructions (see pages 172–180). Stop your trouser-making process before folding the waist edge over. Zigzag-stitch the waist edge.

You now need to cut the bodice pieces for your romper. You are going to use the trouser part you have just made and a close-fitting vest top to mark the shape.

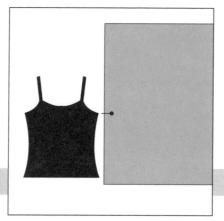 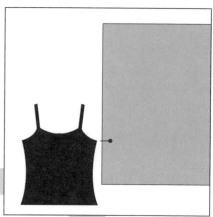

1_ Determine how long the bodice part of your romper will be. The one shown in these instructions is fairly long, causing fabric to hang over at the waist. To make a long bodice, lay your vest top next to, and sitting above the bottom edge of, your fabric. Put a pin in your fabric (or make a chalk mark) level with the armpit point of your vest. This is shown with a purple pin on the illustrations.

You can make an even deeper top, with a bigger overhang, by pushing your vest top further up. If on the other hand you want a tighter-fitting bodice that clings to your chest and reveals your waist, position your vest top so that the bottom sits below the bottom edge of your fabric. The variations on pages 188–189 will help you decide.

 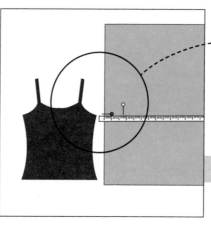 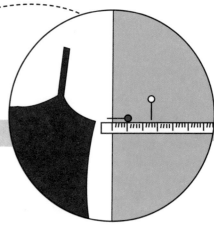

2_ Measure the width of your vest top from armpit point to armpit point. Divide the measurement in half and write it down. You are going to make your bodice piece this much wider than your vest top. Half of the measurement you have just written down will go each side of your vest top, so halve the number again and write that down. We'll call this your **extra width measurement**.

3_ Measure your extra width measurement inwards from the side of your fabric and put a pin in here.

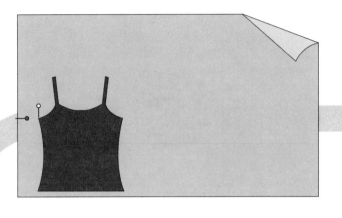

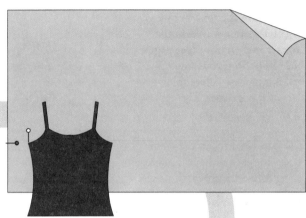

4_ Lay the armpit point of your vest top level
with this pin.

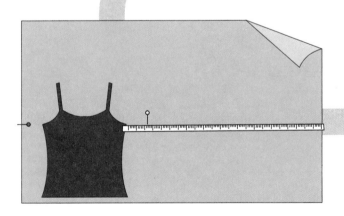

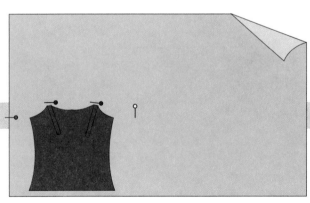

5_ Now measure your extra width
measurement across from your right
armpit point and put a pin in here.

6_ Put pins into your fabric where the straps
of your vest top meet the main body.

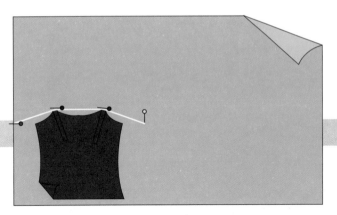

7_ Now draw lines between your pins with tailor's chalk.

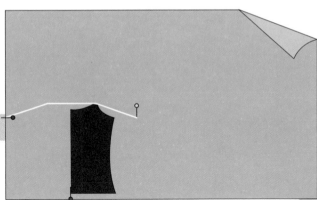

8_ You need to make the bottom edge of your bodice piece exactly the same width as the waist edge of your trousers. To do this accurately, fold your vest top in half where it lies. This will allow you to find the centre of your bodice piece. Put a pin in here.

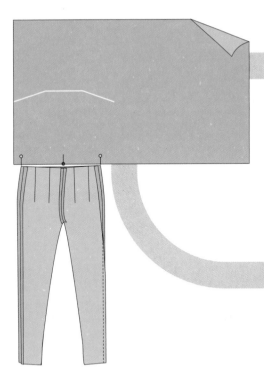

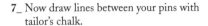

9_ Remove the vest top. With your trousers turned inside out, lay them out below your fabric with the central seam directly below the central pin on your fabric. Put a pin in your fabric level with the sides of your trouser piece at both sides.

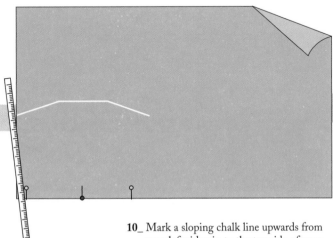

10_ Mark a sloping chalk line upwards from your left side pin to the top side of your bodice piece.

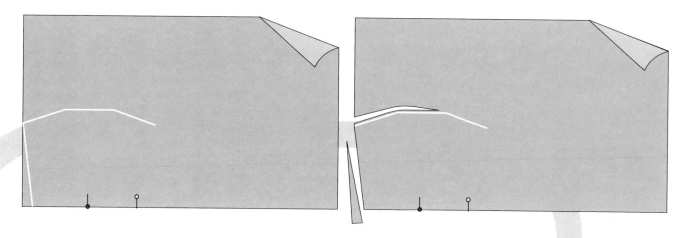

11_ Cut along this line, then cut halfway across the top of your bodice piece.

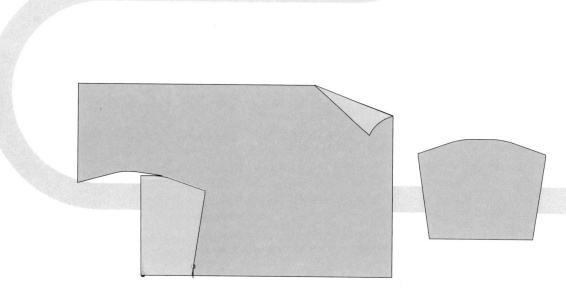

12_ Take this cut half and fold it across to the opposite side. You are going to use your first half as a guide so that your bodice piece is perfectly symmetrical. The most important points to match up are the bottom ones. Make sure the corner of the folded side sits touching the bottom pin.

13_ Cut around this second half. You have made the front of your bodice.

Use your front bodice piece as a guide to mark and cut your back bodice piece.

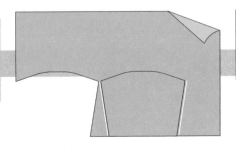

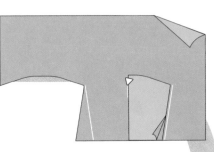

14_ Lay your front bodice piece out on your fabric and use it as a guide to mark the two sloping vertical sides.

15_ Your back piece is going to curve downwards instead of upwards across the top. Fold your front piece in half to find the centre and mark this central axis on your fabric with chalk.

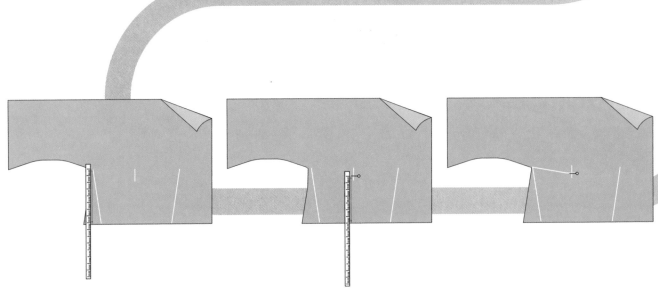

16_ Measure the depth of your back piece from the armpit point down to the bottom edge.

17_ Now move your tape measure to the central axis you have marked and measure that depth minus about 6cm (2½in) up from the bottom of your fabric. Put a pin into your fabric to mark this shorter depth.

18_ Now draw a line that slopes from the taller, outer edge to that pin. This should make a line that slopes gently downwards to the centre of your piece.

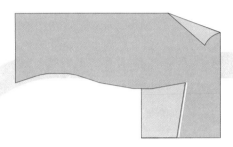

20_ Cut out your piece.

19_ Cut one half of your back piece, then fold it over to the other side so that your piece has an identical slope on each side.

You need to make a strip of facing for the top of each of your bodice pieces. This is going to form a tunnel through which you will thread elastic. It needs to be about 3cm (1¼in) deeper than the elastic you plan to use.

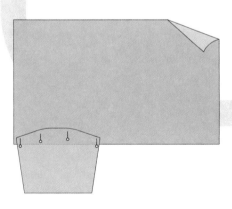

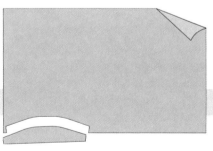

21_ Pin the top edge of your front piece to your fabric and use the edge of it as a guide to cut your facing.

22_ Trim the bottom edge so the line runs parallel with the top edge of your facing and so that the facing is as deep as you need it to be.

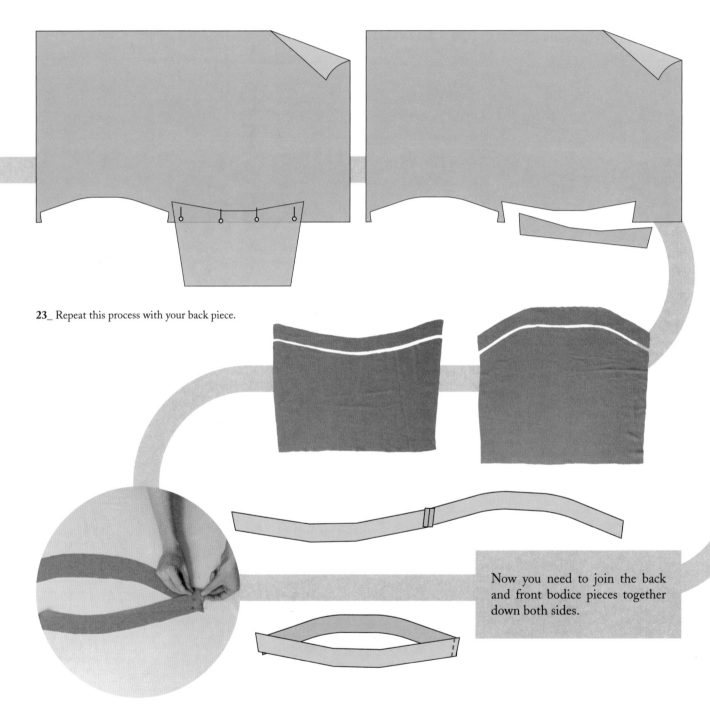

23_ Repeat this process with your back piece.

24_ With right sides together, pin and sew your two pieces of facing together at one side, then iron the seam open.

Now you need to join the back and front bodice pieces together down both sides.

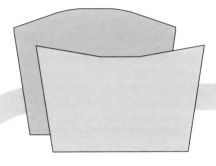

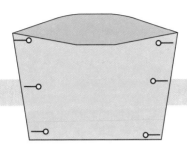

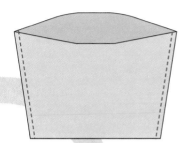

25_ Lay out your front piece with the right side facing upwards and lay your back piece on top of it, with the right side facing down.

26_ Match up the top edges and pin together down each side.

27_ Sew together with straight stitch and iron the seams open.

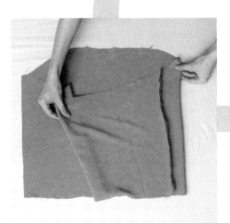

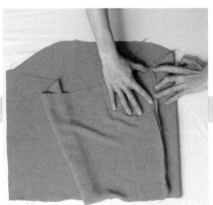

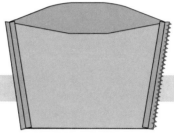

28_ Zigzag-stitch down each of these raw edges.

Next you need to attach your facing to your bodice piece.

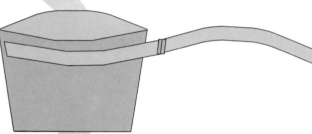

29_ Turn your bodice piece the right way out so that you are looking at the right side of the fabric, and the back of your bodice. Lay your facing out so that it matches the top edge of your back piece. You should be looking at the wrong side of your facing.

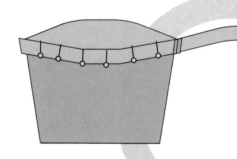

30_ Pin the facing to the top edge of the bodice all the way round.

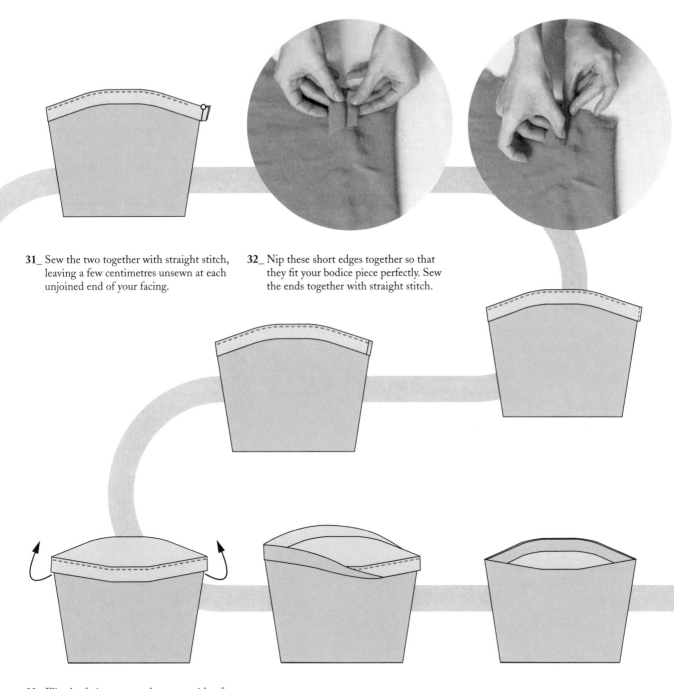

31_ Sew the two together with straight stitch, leaving a few centimetres unsewn at each unjoined end of your facing.

32_ Nip these short edges together so that they fit your bodice piece perfectly. Sew the ends together with straight stitch.

33_ Flip the facing over to the wrong side of your bodice and iron it so that it sits just a millimetre or so below the top edge of your bodice.

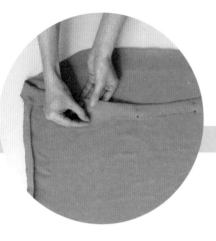

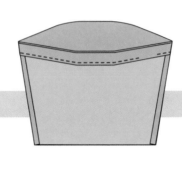

Next, you need to attach your bodice to your trousers.

34_ Turn inside out, pin the facing down well and sew it almost all the way round.

35_ Leave 4 or 5cm (1½–2in) unsewn so that you can push your elastic in later on.

36_ With your bodice inside out and upside down, insert your trousers (the right way round and the right way up) into it. Remember to match back to back and front to front. Your bodice forms a tube. Push your trouser piece up into it so that

the waist edge of your trousers meets the waist edge of your top. They should be the same width. If one is a little bit bigger, sew a line further in from the edge to make it smaller. When the two are exactly the same size, pull the trousers up even further.

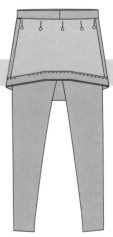

37_ You want your bodice piece to be sitting a few centimetres below the waist edge of your trousers. The amount depends on the width of the elastic you are going to insert at the waist of your romper. If you are inserting a piece of elastic that is 3cm (1¼in) wide, you need to leave an extra

4.5cm (1¾in) of fabric. This allows 1.5cm (⅝in) to make a seam. Pin the top and trousers together all the way around this edge, then sew them together all the way around this pinned line.

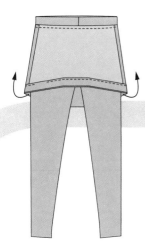

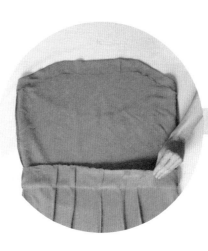

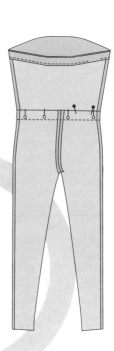

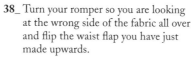

38_ Turn your romper so you are looking at the wrong side of the fabric all over and flip the waist flap you have just made upwards.

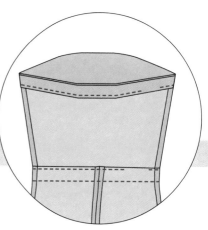

39_ Pin it into position and sew it down almost all the way around.

40_ Make sure you leave a gap so that you will be able to push your elastic in.

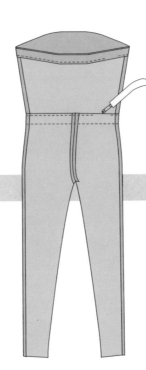

41_ Use a safety pin to work your elastic through the tunnel you have made, as described in the trouser instructions on pages 183–184.

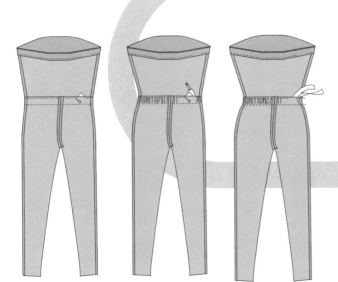

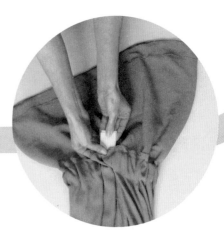

42_ When the end of your elastic emerges again, pin the two ends together and join them with straight stitch.

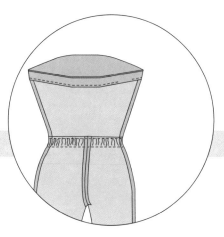

43_ Sew a short row of straight stitch to seal the gap you left open for your elastic.

If you want to add straps to your romper, do it now. See page 19 for instructions.

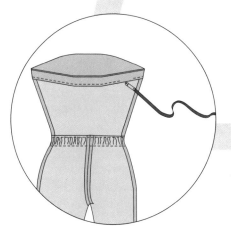

you have made a romper

44_ Repeat this process with your bust elastic. Tie the ends together with plenty of extra elastic and try your romper on. Tighten or loosen the bust elastic while you are wearing it until you have the tension that you want. If you are not adding straps you need the elastic to be tight enough to hold your romper up securely.

templates

These outline drawings show some of the endless garment variations that can be created by following the instructions in this book. Trace them, colour them in, photocopy and cut them up to help you visualize what you would like to make.

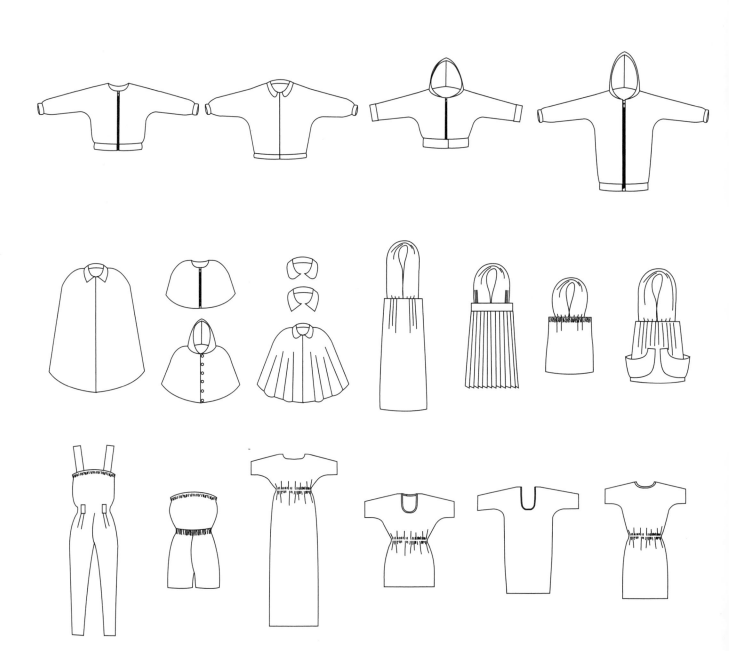

sewing resources

The internet is a great place to turn to if you need help, advice or inspiration for any DIY sewing project.

STARTING OUT AND TECHNICAL TIPS

Here are a few key websites that will get you going.

PatternReview.com

sewing.patternreview.com/SewingMachine/Reviews
If you are buying your first machine and are not sure where to start, this website has a searchable directory of user reviews of a huge range of machines. An extremely useful resource.

The Sewing Forum

www.thesewingforum.co.uk
If you stumble and need help with a specific problem, The Sewing Forum is a wonderful UK site. You need to sign up and make yourself an ID, which is free, then ask any sewing-related question you like and you'll receive a rapid response from an actual human. An amazing resource.

Start Sewing

www.startsewing.co.uk
If you want a few pointers about basic sewing skills this is a clear, well-managed website with videos and written guidance. It aims to be 'a central place with everything you need to know about basic sewing skills and to help you move on to more advanced sewing' and it does a good job.

BLOGGERS

There are some great DIY sewing bloggers, posting photos of simple alteration and make-it-from-scratch projects online. They are stylish, creative, budget-conscious and they are sharing their projects with you for free.

I Spy DIY

'Spot style you love and Do-It-Yourself!'
www.ispy-diy.com
@ISpyDIY

Chic Steals

'Learn how to make the things you covet.'
www.chic-steals.com
@ChicSteals

A Pair And A Spare

'The best DIY fashion inspirations and tutorials.'
www.apair-andaspare.blogspot.com
@apairandaspare

P.S. I made this...

'I see it. I like it. I make it.'
psimadethis.com
@psimadethis